MW00816570

Created for Love

Created for Love

Reflections for the Catholic Bride-to-Be

CHLOE LANGR

OSV

Our Sunday Visitor
Huntington, Indiana

Our Sunday Visitor Publishing Division

Our Sunday Visitor, Inc.

200 Noll Plaza

Huntington, IN 46750

1-800-348-2440

ISBN: 978-1-68192-377-2 (Inventory No. T2263)

LCCN: 2019943401

Cover design: Tyler Ottinger

Cover art: Marie Heimann

Interior design: Amanda Falk

Interior art: Shutterstock

PRINTED IN THE UNITED STATES OF AMERICA

*To Joseph — thank you for always loving
me more today than yesterday.*

CONTENTS

INTRODUCTION

Congratulations! I'm so excited for you and the adventures that Christ has in store for your marriage. You've found the one whom your soul loves, and that's something to celebrate. But as exciting as your upcoming wedding is, planning for that big day can be stressful. You'll quickly find out (if you haven't already!) the many little things that have to be done.

Don't get me wrong — planning a wedding is beautiful and incredibly fun! But it can also be immensely overwhelming. You might feel like the weight of the world is on your shoulders. The to-do list before the wedding day presses in around you. Your mind is swirling with questions about bridesmaid dresses, reception locations, and RSVPs. Your time is eaten up by searching for the perfect dress (mermaid or empire waist?), planning the reception menu (beef or chicken?), and processing expectations from family and friends.

It can be exhausting.

But it doesn't have to be exhausting.

The world tells you to rush through this season of your life. Our culture tells you to set up a countdown timer on your phone and hurry to get ready for the big day. Bridal magazines transform this time into one massive to-do list of things to worry about.

This big day you're planning? It's not about hosting the perfect party. It's about celebrating the vows you're about to make to love the man you have chosen in sickness and in health, on the good days and the bad days, when things run smoothly and when things feel like they are

9

falling apart.

As an engaged woman, it's oh-so-tempting to wrap up your identity in your wedding planning. But your identity rests in something much deeper than your upcoming wedding day. First and foremost, you are a daughter of God.

He created you for love.

He's given you a purpose.

He delights in your feminine genius.

This is not a book about how to pick out the perfect wedding color that will flatter everyone in the bridal party, or how to plan a budget for your big day. This is a journal to give you a space to prepare for the lifetime after the big day. This is a book about preparing your heart and diving deep into your interior life as you get ready to walk to the altar. In this hectic season, I hope this book will be an oasis of beauty to which you will retreat often.

There are big things ahead of you. Your engagement (and your future marriage) offer you an opportunity to grow, to dive headfirst into God's love and discover the source of your identity and your beauty in his heart. Within these pages, you'll find a place to discover your unique, radiant feminine genius.

What is this feminine genius?

In his 1995 "Letter to Women," Pope Saint John Paul II wrote, "It is thus my hope, dear sisters, that you will reflect carefully on what it means to speak of the 'genius of women,' not only in order to be able to see in this phrase a specific part of God's plan which needs to be accepted and appreciated, but also in order to let this genius be more fully expressed in the life of society as a whole, as well as in the life of the Church" (10). This period of engagement is the perfect opportunity to reflect on your unique feminine genius and your incredible calling as a woman, as you prepare to take on the vocation of wife.

Pope Saint John Paul II explains that feminine genius is expressed uniquely in each woman's life in four key ways: receptivity, sensitivity, generosity, and maternity. Every woman, regardless of her state in life or her vocation, is called to live the feminine genius in her own beautifully unrepeatable way.

In these pages, I invite you to press the pause button and take a deep breath. Use this space to reflect and ponder in your heart (as Mary did) as you explore what it means to be a receptive, sensitive, generous, and maternal woman. This book provides space for you to journal, but don't feel that you always have to write when you pick up this book. Some days you may simply need to abide in God's presence, and as you read the reflections included here, let him sing over you with songs of rejoicing. Within these pages you'll also find Scripture to pray with and saints to journey with you.

It may seem counterintuitive, but taking time away from the chaos of wedding planning to recognize your identity as God's daughter will strengthen your future marriage. Far more important than planning the "perfect" day is planting seeds that will grow in your heart. These pages will allow you to document your love story — not just with your future spouse, but also with the God who created you and loves you more than you can possibly imagine. Long after a wedding band adorns your hand, you will be able to look back on this season and rejoice in the plans the Lord has for you and for your marriage.

And sister, he has plans.

On my wedding day, I couldn't imagine loving my husband, Joseph, more than I did then. I couldn't stop looking into his eyes. The next day, my face hurt from smiling so much. But, if I'm being honest, I love him more today than I did on our wedding day. Every morning, when I'm resting in his arms and praying with him, I ask God to give me the grace to love Joseph better today than I did yesterday. Our lives together as the Langr family, I pray, are just beginning.

I know you have a wedding to plan. But remember, a wedding is a day. It's a beautiful, grace-filled, heart-swelling twenty-four hours. But it's just a day. Your marriage? Sister, I'm praying that your marriage will be a lifetime adventure. I can't wait to share this journey with you. Know of my prayers!

In Christ through Mary,
Chloe Langr

THE BRIDE IS
loved
IT IS SHE WHO RECEIVES
love
IN ORDER TO
love
IN RETURN

Part One
Receptivity

*"Behold, I am the handmaid of the Lord; let
it be to me according to your word."*

— Luke 1:38

AN INVITATION
TO RECEIVE

*"Holiness consists simply in doing God's will,
and being just what God wants us to be."*

— Saint Thérèse of Lisieux

As beautiful as your wedding day will be (and it's going to be so beautiful), it's not going to be perfect. If you throw yourself headfirst into creating a perfect wedding day, you'll arrive worn out and exhausted at the altar.

Believe me, I speak from firsthand experience. As soon as I was engaged, I began striving for the perfect wedding day. I have always been a perfectionist, so it wasn't a surprise that I expected perfection from myself when it came to planning my wedding. I stuffed my schedule so full that I'd fall asleep utterly exhausted at three in the morning, still upset that everything wasn't done for the big day yet. But despite knowing that my schedule was full to the max, I'd still say yes to almost anything asked of me.

I imagined myself as a circus juggler, adding more and more balls to my act, testing how long I could keep them in the air. And slowly, as my wedding day came closer and closer, I began to lose my grip.

Everything I was passionate about seemed to be slumping. Work overwhelmed me. My health was in mysterious chaos. My spiritual life hit rock bottom as I went weeks without desiring to pray. Even my wedding, a day when I'd marry the man I loved so dearly, loomed over me dauntingly. I was drained. I walked around in a haze, unable to be energetic about anything, especially around those I loved the most.

Somehow, I had to balance everything and not disappoint anyone who was counting on me. But how could I keep up my pretense of perfection, telling everyone it was fine, when I knew people were starting to glimpse the struggling, broken me? So many nights, I crawled into bed, praying and begging God to show me how to juggle better.

God didn't teach me how to juggle.

He taught me how to let things fall, and then he taught me how to fall into his arms.

Only when I stopped long enough to receive his presence did peace come flowing, slowly but surely, into my wedding planning. Finally, I paused and spent time listening to the Lord's voice.

Right now, I invite you to pause in your to-do list, lay aside whatever is worrying you, and simply be. Receive the Lord's presence in this moment.

This invitation to receptivity flies in the face of our culture's obsession with productivity. But your heart needs to receive the love that the Lord wants to shower down upon you in this season. God is madly in love with you. These pages won't be seen by anyone but you, so don't be afraid to simply show up and let yourself be seen by the Lover of your heart.

Today, give everything about your engagement to him. Pour out everything you're thinking about and processing, from the details of the wedding to your hopes and dreams for your marriage. Let him know what is keeping you from fully surrendering this season to him, and what you're most hesitant to give him.

Ask for the specific graces you need — those you're aware of and those you don't even know — from the Lord in preparation for this sacrament.

Heavenly Father, this season of my life is full of so many voices, pulling me in many directions. Help me to dedicate time to you so that I can listen to the one voice that truly matters — yours. Fill me with the desire to be captivated by you and the love you have for me. Plant in my heart the knowledge that I am your beloved daughter, and teach me to find my identity in you. I promise to intentionally sit and listen for your still, small voice during this season of my engagement.

_____

_____

_____

_____

_____

_____

_____

_____

_____

_____

_____

_____

_____

_____

_____

_____

_____

REJECTING THE LIES

"Yes, there is that voice, the voice that speaks above and from within that whispers soft or declares loudly: 'You are my Beloved, on you my favor rests.' It certainly is not easy to hear that voice in a world filled with voices that shout: 'You are no good, you are ugly; you are worthless; you are despicable, you are nobody — unless you can demonstrate the opposite.'"

— Henri J. M. Nouwen

W e can't be receptive to God's plan for our lives until we weed out the lies the devil sows in our hearts.

Throughout our lives as women striving for the Lord, the devil cunningly urges us to question what God says, to doubt the Father's truths. Instead of rejoicing as his daughters, created for love, we wonder whether we're good enough. We doubt anyone could ever love all of us. We hide away parts of our story that we think make us unworthy of love. We begin to believe that we are responsible for earning the Father's love.

The voice of the Father, reminding us of our inherent worth, has always been there. But his voice begins to sound far off and unconvincing when, day after day, the devil's lies tell us we have to prove our worth. It is easy to let those lies fester in our hearts, digging so deep that we begin to wonder whether those lies actually form our identity.

But the lies don't just destroy our relationship with the Father. The devil's shouting in your ear can make you deaf to those you love the most. In this season of your engagement, you're preparing to enter into a sacrament that makes visible the invisible Trinitarian love of God. It's no wonder that the devil also wants to infiltrate the relationship between you and your fiancé. He wants to distract your heart from love of God and love in your marriage as well.

Don't be afraid to ask the Lord to show you how you might have closed yourself off from his love, where your heart has grown stone-cold. Let him show you where the lies from the devil have made your heart hesitant to be open, afraid of being wounded.

In his Letter to the Ephesians, Saint Paul writes that "but when anything is exposed by the light it becomes visible, for anything that becomes visible is light" (Eph 5:13). As we journey to accept our identity as God's beloved daughters, we start by bringing the devil's lies to light, with God's help.

What negative voices and lies haunt your heart? In what ways have you started to agree with those lies? Take an honest look at what is holding you back from being your authentic self during this season. What is keeping you from living life fully?

Are you worried about what people will think of you?

Do you beat yourself up over even the smallest mistakes?

Do you wonder whether a decision you made in the past makes you unworthy of God's love?

Are you holding yourself, your wedding, and your future marriage up to impossible standards?

Do you think you're the only one struggling with this season of life?

Have you bought into the lie that life will only start after your vows at the altar?

Do you wonder whether you can really trust God, or worry that he isn't who he says he is?

These are only some of the lies that might sneak into your heart.

Make time to think about what specific lies could be holding you back during this season of marriage preparation.

When we name the lies that chain us down, we destroy their power to enslave our hearts and souls. Write down the lies and sins that are holding you back from living in this season as a daughter who is aware that she is beloved, aware that she is created for love. Today, resolve to actively reject these lies. Draw a line through every lie that the devil has sold you. Reject the deceits and falsehoods from the father of lies.

When you're tempted to find your identity in the lies that the devil has whispered in your ear, turn to Christ in prayer and ask him to affirm your true identity as his beloved.

Heavenly Father, you have created me, seen me, and said that I am good. When the devil whispers his lies into my heart, help me courageously bring his deceptions to you, where they can be revealed in your light. Help me to find my identity first and foremost as your beloved, your daughter. Give me the grace of receptivity to be open to your unique call to the depths of my heart.

BE SATISFIED WITH HIM

"Only God can give what the heart wants. In true Christian love, the husband and wife see God coming through their love. But without God the infinity must be sought in the finitude of the partner, which is to gather figs from thistles. Eternity is in the soul, and all the materialism of the world cannot uproot it."

— Archbishop Fulton J. Sheen

After Joseph and I got married, I naively thought that being satisfied with the Lord wouldn't apply anymore. After all, I'd prayed for satisfaction when I was single. I had worked on finding that intensely personal and unique relationship with Christ, and then he introduced Joseph and me and led us toward our vocation together.

But even though I had discerned marriage with a man whom I love and who leads me closer to Christ, I quickly found out that Joseph was not called to satisfy me. And I couldn't satisfy him. We were both messy human beings who couldn't fulfill the role that Christ was supposed to have in our lives.

Marriage, even though it is beautiful and good, can't answer the desires of my heart and my yearning for an unconditional love. Expecting

Joseph to fulfill and satisfy my every need was expecting my husband to fill the God-shaped hole in my heart.

Are you satisfied with Christ alone? Or are you constantly looking for another source of fulfillment?

Don't get stuck waiting for the "next" in each stage of your life. I spent too much time as a single woman waiting for the "next" of being in a relationship. When Joseph and I were dating, I couldn't wait for the "next" of engagement. Our season of engagement found me longing for the "next" of married life together. I was so excited to get to say good-night instead of goodbye at the end of the evening. Then, I thought that the only thing that could make me happier than being married was being a mother, and I waited for that "next," too. But that constant craving for the "next" quickly stopped me from being satisfied by the joys of the here and now. As I've stopped looking around the corner and instead focused on the Lord's gifts to me in the present moment, I've found that happiness is much more possible.

Be satisfied with Christ, and believe that his plan for your life is better than your wildest dreams. Although your life may not look like what you wanted, his plan is good — even when we don't understand it. Trust him and be satisfied with him. Jesus isn't going to disappoint you.

What areas of your life are you afraid to give to God because you're worried that he won't satisfy them? Today, surrender those areas of your life to the Father. He knows the desires of your heart; he wants to satiate your deepest longings.

As you journal and pray, ask for the grace of confidence. The Father created you for love, and he will not leave you empty.

Everyone longs to give themselves completely to some- one, to have a deep soul relationship with another, to be loved thoroughly and exclusively. But to a Christian, God says, No, not until you are satisfied, fulfilled, and con- tent with being loved by me alone, with giving yourself totally and unreservedly to me, with having an intensely

personal and unique relationship with me alone. Discovering that only in me is your satisfaction to be found, will you be capable of the perfect human relationship that I have planned for you. You will never be united to another until you are united with me alone. Exclusive of anyone or anything else. Exclusive of any other desires or longings. I want you to stop planning, to stop wishing, and allow me to give you the most thrilling plan existing ... one that you cannot imagine. I want you to have the best. Please allow me to bring it to you. You just keep watching me, expecting the greatest things. Keep experiencing the satisfaction that I am. Keep listening and learning the things that I tell you. You just wait. That's all. Don't be anxious; don't worry. Don't look around at the things you think you want. You just keep looking off and away up to me, or you'll miss what I want to show you. And then, when you're ready, I'll surprise you with a love far more wonderful than any you could dream of.

And this is the perfect love.

And dear one, I want you to have this most wonderful love; I want you to see in the flesh a picture of your relationship with me. And to enjoy materially and concretely the everlasting union of beauty, perfection, and love that I offer you with myself. Know that I love you utterly. I AM God. Believe it and be satisfied. (author unknown)

_____

_____

_____

_____

_____

_____

_____

_____

_____

_____

_____

_____

_____

_____

_____

_____

HEARING THE
FATHER'S SONGS

"The Lord, your God, is in your midst, a warrior who
gives victory; he will rejoice over you with gladness,
he will renew you in his love; he will exult over you
with loud singing as on a day of festival."

— Zephaniah 3:17–18

Imagine that on your wedding day you spend a few quiet, precious minutes with your husband-to-be. Excitedly, you give him a gift that you selected and wrapped with care. Brimming with excitement, you watch as he opens your gift. He turns it over in his hands, looks at it closely, but there isn't a smile on his face. He doesn't share your excitement. Instead, he turns to you and says, "Thank you for thinking of me, but this isn't really something I want. Here, you can have it back."

Can you imagine how sadly his response would echo in your heart?

I pray that never happens to you — especially on your wedding day! Yet, when we don't accept the beautiful way that the Lord has created us, we reject a gift that the Lord has picked out intentionally for us. He gives us a set of gifts unique to our very person. But how often do we cast off his gifts, shrugging them off as something we don't want or need? He sings over our life with a song of rejoicing, but we often want to plug our ears, blocking out the Lord's voice.

What makes the Lord rejoice over you? What things about you make you uniquely, beautifully you? Is it the way that you laugh? The way that your eyes light up at the sight of a sunrise? Your talents as an organizer? How you wake up slowly in the morning?

How has God created you for love? Do you pay attention to the little things in the lives of those you love? Are you eager to lend a hand when you see someone in need? Do you have a gift for remembering small details and making people feel known? Can the people in your life turn to you when they need a shoulder to cry on, or an ear to listen?

In what unique ways do you love in your relationship with the Lord? Is it the way that you strive to serve God with your entire heart, soul, and mind? How you see others with your heart? Your ability to patiently exist in this season of waiting, knowing that the Lord is in the present moment?

We call out the devil's lies in our hearts, bringing them into the light. So too, we need to take time to call out and rejoice in the truths that God has woven into our very beings. The real way that we discover our beauty as women, and as brides, is to be receptive of these truths and his love.

Father, thank you for creating me — all of me. Thank you for the truths that you've spoken into my heart, for how you've woven my very being. Too often, the world tries to stifle and smother the truths that you sing over me. Give me the grace to focus attentively on your loving voice in the midst of the chaos. Help me to abide in the truth of who I am in you.

_____

_____

_____

_____

_____

_____

_____

_____

_____

_____

_____

_____

_____

_____

_____

_____

TRUSTING THE GIVER

"The secret of happiness is to live moment by moment and to thank God for all that He, in His goodness, sends to us day after day."

— Saint Gianna Molla

L ittle kids can be the best gift-givers. When I spent the summer babysitting for the kids in my neighborhood, the littles would run up to me, their hands behind their backs. "We have a gift for you!" they'd exclaim, giggling and exchanging sneaky glances among themselves. "Open up your hands! Close your eyes!"

But instead of willingly opening my hands and closing my eyes in a moment of trust, I hesitated. What could they be hiding? A thoughtful picture they drew that they can't wait to interpret, or a little bug they found crawling around in the backyard?

Their giggles and conspiratorial glances made me both excited and nervous. But my hesitancy truly boiled down to this one truth: I didn't know whether I could trust their gifts. I might open my hands and close my eyes, only to look down and see something squirmy, squiggly, and squishy in my palms. Or I might be pleasantly surprised. It was a gamble. My hesitancy closed off my heart to their little gifts.

God isn't like that when it comes to showering us with gifts. We can trust him — we don't have to be afraid.

What facets of wedding planning are you afraid of or nervous about? Perhaps you're worried about a family member's expectations for the day. Maybe you're struggling with comparing your wedding to the weddings of other women around you.

Today, give that particular struggle over to the Lord and let go of it. Approach with your palms open, receptive to his will in the situation. Trust that he will give you the gifts your heart desires.

What are your hopes for not only your wedding day, but also your marriage? What do you hope will come to fulfillment on the day of your wedding? List the parts of the day, and of your approaching vocation, that you're looking forward to the most. Describe the dreams, no matter how small or large.

Now take a few minutes to rest in the knowledge that God is a good father. He is going to show up when you invite him in. Rejoice, knowing that he's going to keep his promises, and give those hopes and dreams to him. After looking through all of your plans, give them one by one to the Lord. Pray for the grace to be open and receptive to his will for your wedding day and for your marriage — especially if his plan looks different than the one you just wrote down.

Holy Spirit, you know my heart. You see my fears in this particular area of the planning. Help me give you permission to operate outside of my paradigm for the wedding day. Encourage a spirit of receptivity in my heart so that I can grow even more into the woman, the bride, that you have created me to be. Heavenly Father, help me rest in the knowledge that you do not give your children stones when they ask for bread, but instead fill them up with good things. Lord, you know the desires of my heart. Help me to want what you desire for me, and to be receptive

to your plan — especially when it looks different than I expected.

_____

_____

_____

_____

_____

_____

_____

_____

_____

_____

_____

_____

_____

_____

RECEPTIVITY REVEALED IN OUR BODIES

"The body, and it alone, is capable of making visible what is invisible: the spiritual and the divine. It was created to transfer into the visible reality of the world the mystery hidden since time immemorial in God [God's love for man], and thus be a sign of it."

— Pope Saint John Paul II

Not only is receptivity something that we're called to live in our spiritual and emotional lives as women, but receptivity is also stamped into our very bodies.

Thanks to advertisements, Photoshop, and unrealistic expectations for women's bodies, it can be hard to believe that God created our bodies and calls them good. Instead, we're tempted to focus on how our bodies don't match up to the world's standard of beauty.

But sister, your body is good. Your body is holy. Your body is sacramental — it reveals the reality of the way Christ loves us to the world. In a world of unrealistic expectations, your body reveals a mystery.

But just what is that?

It's the same mystery that Saint Paul talks about in his Letter to the Ephesians. After teaching about the beauty of a married man and woman, Paul says, "This is a great mystery, and I mean in reference to Christ and the Church" (Eph 5:32).

If Christ is the bridegroom, his bride is the Church, made up of all Christian men and women. In *Mulieris Dignitatem*, his apostolic letter "On the Dignity and Vocation of Women" published August 15, 1988, Pope Saint John Paul II described the beauty of this relationship when he wrote, "The Bridegroom is the one who loves. The Bride is loved: It is she who receives love, in order to love in return."

Our bodies are made for reception. In the sexual act we receive our husbands. If God wills it, we also receive the gift of new life within our wombs. Our receptive bodies are a sign to the world of the love of the Father. Our bodies reveal that all human beings are invited to receive.

"Holy women ... are also a model for all Christians ... an example of how the Bride must respond with love to the love of the Bridegroom," Pope Saint John Paul II said in *Mulieris Dignitatem*. He described this incarnation as "a special kind of 'prophetism' that belongs to women in their femininity. The analogy of the Bridegroom and the Bride speaks of the love with which every human being — man and woman — is loved by God in Christ. But in the context of the biblical analogy ... it is precisely the woman — the bride — who manifests this truth to everyone."

In your marriage, your bodies reflect the intentional design of God. Your union reveals to the world the union between God and humanity, and your feminine body reveals to the world that we are called to be receptive to the love of the Father, who created us all for love.

How will your marriage uniquely reflect this divine relationship? In what way can your receptivity invite your fiancé to participate in the receptivity we're called to as sons and daughters of God?

Father, in your wisdom, you've created my body to reveal the beauty of receptivity to the world and those around

me. Help me to revel in that truth and to intentionally reveal your gifts to the world.

_____

_____

_____

_____

_____

_____

_____

_____

_____

_____

_____

_____

_____

MARY AT THE ANNUNCIATION

"But when the time had fully come, God sent forth his Son, born of woman, born under the law, to redeem those who were under the law, so that we might receive adoption as sons."

— Galatians 4:4–5

"Hail, full of grace, the Lord is with you!" Can you imagine Mary's reactions to these words that Gabriel spoke to her (Lk 1:28)? How would you react if an angel of the Lord appeared before you and sang your praises?

Mary's reaction was understandable. She was greatly troubled — and can you blame her? An angel was standing in front of her, explaining how she, a virgin, would give birth to the Son of God.

God didn't force Mary to say yes to the mission that he invited her into. Instead, he waited for her to help him become man. But God wasn't the only one who waited eagerly for Mary's response.

"Tearful Adam with his sorrowing family begs this of you, O loving Virgin, in their exile from Paradise. Abraham begs it, David begs it. All the other holy patriarchs, your ancestors, ask it of you, as they dwell in the country of the shadow of death. This is what the whole earth waits for, prostrate at your feet," Saint Bernard of Clairvaux wrote in his meditation on the Annunciation.

Heaven and earth, saints and angels, waited with bated breath to see what Mary would say to this invitation. The Desire of Nations awaits at the door to Mary's heart, listening for her response. "Arise, hasten, open. Arise in faith, hasten in devotion, open in praise and thanksgiving," Saint Bernard continued.

Maybe, in the silence of that moment, Mary took a deep breath. Perhaps she closed her eyes for a minute. But then she responded with her fiat. Her words echo throughout all of time: "Behold, I am the handmaid of the Lord; let it be to me according to your word" (Lk 1:38).

Through Mary's receptivity, Christ enters the world as a human baby. Without sin clouding her vision, Mary joyfully responds with a generous, receptive "yes."

Eve, the original woman, was created in the garden with the same capacity for an unrestrained, joyful "yes" to the Lord's plan. But instead of responding with receptivity and trust, Eve grasped at her own plans. Instead of proclaiming a fiat, Eve responded with fear.

While Mary's fiat echoes throughout all of time, Eve's fearful grasping still affects each of our lives and hearts as women today. Because of that original sin, how easy it is for us as women today to close our hearts to God's plan, responding with fear instead of a fiat.

But Mary's receptivity and openness allowed Christ, responding to that receptivity, to give us the gift of eternal salvation. Eve's name means "mother of all living," but Mary, the new Eve, becomes a mother to all of us who experience abundant life thanks to Christ's sacrifice on the cross.

Sin mangles our hearts. Instead of our original openness and receptivity, we can be tempted to close ourselves off from God's plan. But Christ waits for your "yes" to his mission for you and for your marriage. He invites you to help bring his life into this world — a world that longs to see what love really means. What is one thing you can do today to open your heart to be a little more receptive? Ask the Blessed Mother's help to be open to God's will for your life.

Heavenly Father, you waited for Mary's beautiful, radical, receptive "yes" to your invitation. Help me to pause in the busyness of this season to listen to the invitation that you offer me and the mission you desire for my marriage. Help me respond with the same generous receptivity that you inspired in the heart of the Blessed Mother. Mary, be with me on this journey to the altar, but also on this journey to the heart of your Son. Help me to not be afraid of his invitation.

_____

_____

_____

_____

_____

_____

_____

_____

_____

A RADICAL MISSION
TO LOVE

*"If a man and a woman marry in order to be companions
on the journey from earth to heaven, then their union
will bring great joy to themselves and to others."*

— Saint John Chrysostom

Growing up, every time I heard that wives should be submissive to their husbands as to the Lord from the pulpit at Mass, I squirmed in my seat a little. Something didn't quite sound right with the word submission. It sounded archaic, but also like an encouragement from Saint Paul to lay down, be a doormat, and let the husband dominate.

If that's what Saint Paul meant in his Letter to the Ephesians (5:22–33), I'd have every right to squirm at his words. And, unfortunately, some men have used Paul's words to justify their twisted desire to control the women in their lives. But that wasn't how Paul intended his words to be read. It wasn't until a few months before my wedding that I found out the true meaning of the word *submission*.

Paul first calls husbands and wives to be subject to one another "out of reverence for Christ." Paul didn't mean that women are worth less than their husbands, or that women should be enslaved to their spouses. Your ability to love your soon-to-be husband (and his ability to love you) "depends on his willingness consciously to seek a good together with others, and to subordinate himself to that good for the sake of others, or to others for the sake of that good," Pope Saint John Paul II wrote in his book *Love and Responsibility*.

Then I took a closer look at the word *submission*. "Sub" means under — think about how submarines go under the water. The Christian understanding of the word *mission* refers to the vocation, or calling, that Christ gives each and every one of us to go out into the world and spread the Gospel. Instead of an invitation to be a doormat, Saint Paul extends to women an invitation to be under the mission of our spouses. And what is that? Your husband's mission is a radical mission to love you.

"You want your wife to obey you as the Church obeys Christ? Then you must care for her as much as Christ cares for the Church," Saint John Chrysostom wrote. "Should it be necessary to die for her, to be cut into a thousand pieces, to bear any sort of suffering, you should not say no."

Husbands are called to love their wives in the same way that Christ loved the Church. How did the Lord love the Church? He took all her burdens upon his shoulders. He bore on his back the heavy cross, trudging slowly, step by step, up to Calvary. He gave his face to spitting, and took all of the insults that were thrown at him. Then, he hung on the cross in agony for three hours, suffering because he would rather die than risk losing the chance to spend all of eternity with each and every one of us. He loved his bride, and he loved her until the end.

That's a mission I can support.

What comes to mind when you think of the word *submission*? Write out your thoughts on your mission as a woman below. What are ways that you can be under the mission of your soon-to-be husband and spread the Gospel together?

Lord, you invite me under the mission of my future spouse. Please reveal to him that his mission is to love me with a crucifixion love, a love that lays down its life in sacrifice for me. But also help me to get behind that mission and to learn how to love as radically in return.

_____

_____

_____

_____

_____

_____

_____

_____

_____

_____

_____

_____

RECEPTIVITY TO
GOD'S GIFTS

"God is always trying to give good things to us,
but our hands are too full to receive them."

— Saint Augustine

I know what it is like to have my hands too full of stuff to receive God's blessings.

One day of wedding preparation left me feeling particularly overwhelmed. It seemed like nothing was going right. Joseph and I couldn't decide what food we were going to serve for the reception. Details about our wedding Mass weren't coming together. Thanks to stress from other areas of our lives, we started to bicker about small details of the wedding.

I walked over to a friend's house that afternoon, hoping for someone to listen to all of my problems and maybe offer a few suggestions.

"What are you thankful for?" my friend asked me, after patiently listening to me vent.

I stared at her. Had she heard a thing I said? I paused for a minute, trying to think of just one thing I was thankful for. "I'm thankful that ... I'm breathing?" I said, ashamed that that was the best I could come up with. She smiled at me.

"I think you should go take a thankful walk," she suggested. She told me to go around the block and, with every step, thank God for something. I grudgingly got up from the couch, stomped out of the door, and sighed. But I took her advice with that first step, and thanked God for my friendship with her. Then I took another step, and thanked God for the blue sky that day. With another step, I thanked him for the fact that I was healthy.

As I replaced my complaints with words of thanks, I stopped stomping through my walk. With each "thank-you" that I breathed out as I walked, I slowed down. I wasn't rushing to get back to all the things that were going wrong with the wedding planning. Instead, I was savoring each step, carefully thinking about what I wanted to thank the Lord for.

By the time I made it around the block, my complaints didn't seem as big. That isn't to say that the conflicts I was stressed about had disappeared. But after my "thankful walk," I was looking at them through a different lens.

In the months ahead, you'll write your fair share of thank-you notes. Between the bridal showers, bachelorette parties, and wedding gifts, you may end up hoping you never have to write another thank-you note again. But before you thank those who have showered you with gifts or their presence, take time to write a thank-you note to God for the ways he has blessed you.

Lord, it's hard to wrap my mind around all of the gifts that you have given me. Thank you. Thank you for what you have withheld, knowing that better things were in store. Thank you for the blessings that you have permitted, as well as the evils you have prevented. Thank you for sacrificing your only begotten Son so that I could spend eternity with you. Thank you for the place in

heaven that you have prepared for me, and for the way that you wait for my response and "yes" to your plan for my life. Thank you for creating me and for loving me from the beginning of time.

_____

_____

_____

_____

_____

_____

_____

_____

_____

_____

_____

_____

_____

YOU ARE ENOUGH

*"The communion of persons means existing in a mutual
'for,' in a relationship of mutual gift. This relationship is
precisely the fulfillment of man's original solitude."*

— Pope Saint John Paul II

The night of our wedding, Joseph and I drove back to our new apartment together. Our reception had been a beautiful night of friends,
food, and great dancing. But we were excited to give our bodies to each
other freely, totally, faithfully, and fruitfully as husband and wife, so we
headed home before the party was over.

I went to the bathroom to take off my makeup, and remembered
a note that my friend had given me the night of my bachelorette party.
I had tucked it under our bathroom sink so that I could read it before
making love with Joseph for the first time.

As I cleaned my face, I thought back to the night of the bachelorette
party. Almost everyone had left after spending a whole day together, but
one of my dearest friends and bridesmaids spent the night with me. We
stayed up until the wee hours, reminiscing about our friendship and
dreaming about the changes ahead in both of our lives. Then, the con-

versation turned from the wedding day to the wedding night. She asked me whether I was nervous.

When I was a teenager, I decided to save sex for marriage. I didn't make that decision out of fear. My decision wasn't because I thought that sex was bad or dirty. But I also realized that if I was called to marriage, I'd come to my wedding night without any sexual experience. I would have been lying if I'd said I wasn't nervous.

Today, sex seems to jump out of every magazine, movie plot line, and billboard. In light of how sexualized our culture is, waiting for marriage can seem prudish and old-fashioned.

I knew that my sex life with Joseph wouldn't automatically be more physically fulfilling because we waited until our wedding night to be together. After all, practicing chastity does not necessarily make you better in bed.

But our bodies and souls weren't just made for physically satisfying sex. Marriage is a context for sex that is holy. Intimacy that honors both your spouse and the Lord only comes within the context of marriage. Your vowed commitment before God and witnesses does make a difference when it comes to your sex life. Sexuality and intimacy are a mystery that we get to spend our entire marriage unraveling — it's not something that we have to have figured out by the time the wedding night rolls around.

That night, I shared everything that was on my heart with my friend. She gave me a piece of journal paper, an envelope, and a pen. Smiling, she asked me to write down everything that I was excited for, hopeful for, and worried about. Then I sealed the envelope and gave it to her.

When I put that envelope in her hands, I realized that all of the things I'd written down in that letter were things that God knew about my heart. He knew how excited I was to give myself to Joseph. He knew what worried me, and what I couldn't wait for. But he wasn't bound by my expectations for that night. Instead, he asked me to simply be receptive to his plan for my marriage, and to surrender my plans to him.

After I gave my letter to her, my friend gave me another envelope. She asked me to read it on the night of Joseph's and my wedding.

"Don't worry, it won't take much time to read," she assured me. So, standing in my bathroom on my wedding night, I pulled out the letter and read it. It was simple, but powerful.

It read: "Dearest daughter — you are enough. Love, God."

Sister, you're enough. The Father created you for love. And, most importantly, you're his daughter.

Today, write a letter to yourself about your wedding night. What are your dreams? Your fears? Your hopes? Then, after writing your heart, ask the Lord for the graces of receptivity, honesty, and passion. He has so many beautiful plans for your marriage and for your wedding night.

Lord, thank you for looking upon me with joy. The world and the devil try to sneak into my heart, seeking to isolate me from you. It's easy to fall into the trap of thinking I'm not beautiful, good, smart, or successful enough. But you don't make mistakes. I praise you because I am fearfully and wonderfully made. Today, help me realize that I am enough, and that nothing can change that truth.

_____

_____

_____

_____

_____

_____

SHE GIVES OF
her best
EVERYWHERE ADDING
A TOUCH OF
generosity,
TENDERNESS,
—AND—
joy of life

Part Two
Generosity

"Thank you, women who are daughters and women who are sisters! Into the heart of the family, and then of all society, you bring the richness of your sensitivity, your intuitiveness, your generosity and fidelity."

— Pope Saint John Paul II

GENEROSITY DOESN'T
MEAN MORE BUSYNESS

*"It is such a folly to pass one's time fretting, instead
of resting quietly on the heart of Jesus."*

— Saint Thérèse of Lisieux

When you opened this section on generosity, were you nervous?
Sometimes when people urge us to be generous, what we hear is,
"Here's one more thing to add to your to-do list." As a bride preparing
for her wedding day, those are the last words you want to hear!

But generosity isn't only about the actions we take. Having a generous spirit means we encounter others and interact with them as Christ
interacts with and loves us. But in order to do that, we have to radically
change our understanding of generosity.

Too often, we think of generosity as a physical or financial response
to disasters in our lives and the lives of those around us. We donate
to the hurricane relief food drive, or drop an envelope in the offertory
collection during Missionary Sunday. Maybe you sponsor a child in a
Third World country, or donate to a local organization that builds up

your community.

It is good to give generously from the tangible gifts God has blessed us with. Christ himself encourages his disciples to tithe at their temple. That kind of charitable generosity flies in the face of a consumer-driven culture that encourages us to watch out for ourselves and no one else. But a bride who knows she was created for love knows that generosity should go much deeper than her pantry or her purse.

Generosity is a heart issue. When he walked on this earth, Christ encouraged generous gift of self in the lives of his disciples. He didn't just ask his followers to donate to a fund, or even to give up their plans for their lives, but to give him their very lives.

The Lord invites us as Catholic women to a generous giving of ourselves — who we are — through intimate friendship and relationship with him and with those around us.

In your marriage, God also invites you to give your future husband not just a part of your life together, some of your joys, and a little of your sorrows, but your whole self — a total gift.

This countercultural generosity is a virtue that requires practice, though. How can we embed generosity in our hearts so that it guides our thoughts, decisions, and actions? How can you give of yourself when you're worried there isn't much left of you to give?

You can begin with asking the Lord to show you where and to whom he desires you to give of yourself. Then, start practicing generosity with small steps. This generous way of life, a total gift of yourself, isn't always seen in broad, sweeping gestures. Instead, it flourishes in the little moments of the day when you pause and choose to encounter someone as the beloved daughter or son of God that they are.

Has your busyness caused you to overlook someone in your life? Have you rushed past someone recently instead of pausing to encounter them? Have you only given the bare minimum in a conversation with a friend or your fiancé lately?

Today, reflect on how you can be generous in the life you're living. Write down a plan for how you can leave time in your schedule this week for generous giving of yourself to others.

This doesn't mean you have to carve out hours of free time and wait for someone to whom you can be generous. Instead, growing a generous heart starts by being intentionally present to those you interact with today and tomorrow and the next day. Maybe you're headed to a wedding dress fitting soon. Make sure to encounter the people at the bridal shop in the way that Christ would encounter them. Perhaps you're asking the women in your life to join you at the altar as your bridesmaids. Choose to be fully present to them in that moment, even setting aside time from wedding preparation to encounter them and share your friendship.

Lord, I can sometimes be afraid when you ask me to give. Some days, the busyness of this season weighs on my shoulders, and I wonder just how much I can really take on before things start to fall apart. Help me trust you when you invite me to give of myself. Help me realize that this invitation isn't something to add to my to-do list, but rather a way of life in which you encourage me to walk alongside you. Give me the grace to generously respond when you show me an opportunity to model your example of loving encounter.

_____

_____

_____

_____

_____

_____

BE GENEROUS
WITH YOURSELF

*"He invites each of us to see the story that our body is
telling, leading us to the place where we can truly say:
'My body is good, and I love the story that it tells.'"*

— Amanda Martinez Beck

Wedding planning isn't for the faint of heart — and neither is marriage! It's no easy task coordinating plans for the big day and
preparing for your vocation. I've been there!

When I was engaged, I remember feeling pulled in so many directions. Ten months seemed like plenty of time to plan, but there were so
many more decisions to make than we had anticipated.

I thought I was handling all the stress like a champ; but looking
back over that season of my life, I now realize I was only kidding myself.

In between crossing things off the list, I spent some time with a dear
friend. On a quiet drive through country fields, we had a heart-to-heart
conversation about how our lives were changing. Before I knew it, we
were delving into some pretty personal subjects. I shared with her how I

felt tired all the time and struggled to see myself as beautiful.

She looked over at me from the passenger seat of my car and, with eyes full of empathy, said, "You don't look healthy. You've lost a lot of weight, and I'm worried about you." I spilled out everything on my heart.

I'd lost fifteen pounds in a few short months. Between wedding planning, packing up my home to move to a new city, and looking for a job, I'd stopped eating. I neglected healthy eating habits so much that my body forgot to tell me when I should have been hungry. I would skip breakfast, substituting a tall cup of coffee for the first meal of the day. I'd skip lunch. Then I'd skip dinner. I would get home around ten most nights and realize that I had eaten almost nothing since the night before.

When I tried on my wedding dress for the last time before the big day, all that I noticed was how different it looked from when I'd first tried it on nine months earlier.

Something had to change. Despite the world telling me that my new slim frame was what I should want, it wasn't what I needed. I needed a balanced life. I needed to be generous with myself and my needs.

What do you think of when you hear the phrase "self-care"? A manicure at your favorite day spa? Sneaking in a bit of chocolate after dinner as a treat?

The world tries to sell us a selfish, commercialized version of self-care. But being generous with and taking care of ourselves goes much deeper than our skin-care routine. True, holistic self-care recognizes that we are both body and soul, created for love. It means loving ourselves as daughters of God, and thanking him for his generosity in creating us. He doesn't make mistakes!

"The question we need to give ourselves permission to ask is not how to feel better, freer, recognized, heard, or seen for a moment over a coffee date or a spa massage, but how to feel whole and genuinely loved inside the skin of our bodies and the depths of our souls — intellect, will, and passions," writes Colleen Mitchell in her book *When We Were Eve: Uncovering the Woman God Created You to Be.* By committing to holistic self-care that appreciates every aspect of our humanity, we actually are praising God, becoming better stewards of the gifts he's given us.

Today, let's make a different kind of gift registry than the one you filled out at Target or Bed Bath and Beyond. There's not a fun pricing gun or aisles to browse through, but this list is even more important than the list of towels and dishes you may have put together.

When will you find time during this hectic season to rest and abide in the Lord with this journal? Pencil it in, just like you would schedule a meeting with your caterer or wedding planner.

Then, think about the other things that you need to give yourself in order to be fully alive and present in this season.

Are you constantly running on fumes, those last details pushing your bedtime later and later? Can you commit to a bedtime routine that honors your body and rests your mind?

Do you often give into the negative voice inside your head that tells you that you're not good enough, or that you'll only be beautiful when you look like the world's standard of bridal beauty? How can you generously and gently challenge yourself to seek out the truth about the woman God has created you to be?

Do you find yourself worrying about the future, how you'll make the lifestyle changes that marriage offers? Can you give yourself time and space to live in the present moment by making time for silence or deep breathing?

When you generously give yourself the things that you've written down in this gift registry, you'll be able to come to the wedding altar full of the Lord's gifts for you.

Father, you've created me for love, and you call me good. Help me to view myself through your loving, generous eyes and recognize my worthiness as your daughter. Inspire me to reject the world's understanding of self-care and instead to realize that authentically loving myself is a direct response to the love you show me on a daily basis.

GENEROUS FORGIVENESS

"To be a Christian means to forgive the inexcusable
because God has forgiven the inexcusable in you."

— C. S. Lewis

Planning a wedding can be a beautiful, messy experience. The day that you'll give yourself to your husband is joyful and exciting, but weddings can also stir up a lot of hurt.

Relationships with friends shift as you prepare to pursue your vocation with your soon-to-be husband. Your expectations for the day may not match your fiancé's desires. Maybe members of either side of the family (or both!) are causing you more stress than you anticipated when you said yes to an engagement ring. When you mention your plans for the ceremony, people may offer their well-intentioned, but sometimes hurtful, opinions.

Take a breath and a step away from the wedding plans. For a few minutes today, leave behind your expectations about what the big day should look, sound, and feel like. After all, not every stage of the wedding planning (nor the actual day!) is going to be Instagram or Pinterest perfect. Instead, it will be a celebration of your new marriage and a celebration of the people who helped you get to the altar.

But people can be messy sometimes, can't they? We're called to love others by willing their good, but we can get hurt along the way. Don't believe me? Look back to Christ on the cross, that perfect image of love — bloody, beaten, and bruised by the people whose sins he is dying for.

From the cross, Christ called out, "Father, forgive them; for they know not what they do" (Lk 23:34). This is the ultimate example of generous forgiveness — forgiving even those who don't realize that they've hurt you. This requires the courage to stop waiting for an apology, and instead to respond to someone who's hurt you with the same kind of forgiveness Christ offers us.

So how can you love others well, especially in this season of engagement? Begin by willing their good. Too often, we think of love as an emotional response to other people, or just a feeling. And when we're hurt, it's easy to not feel love for someone. But love isn't just an emotion — it's a decision, something we actively participate in. Generosity and the choice to love help us to desire the good of the other person, even when our emotions say the opposite.

"So if you are offering your gift at the altar, and there remember that your brother has something against you, leave your gift there before the altar and go; first be reconciled to your brother, and then come and offer your gift," Matthew writes (5:23–24).

Now, I'm not recommending that you wait until you're at the altar in a wedding gown, and then leave to make reparation toward those whom you've hurt and those who've hurt you. You can start forgiving generously and willing their good right now, so that you can come to the wedding altar reconciled and ready to love.

Learning to love and forgive those who have hurt you during this season of engagement is also a beautiful way to practice the forgiveness that is necessary for a fruitful marriage. When you and your fiancé marry, you'll vow to love each other in good times, and in bad times, too. The more authentic and vulnerable you are with each other, the more you open yourself to hurting each other and to being hurt by each other.

Marriage quickly showed me how selfish I could be. I wanted things done my way, and I was hesitant to consider new ideas. So in those first few months of marriage, I found myself asking for forgiveness quite a bit. The greater your capacity for loving someone, the more deeply they can hurt your heart. But this also allows for beautiful opportunities to reflect the generous forgiveness that Christ offers us from the cross.

Today, take the time to make another list. Write down the names of people in your life who have hurt you, especially during this season of preparation. You might find yourself remembering family members who've insulted you, friends who have disappointed you, or someone who made a moment especially difficult.

But don't stop at just writing down their names. Beside their names, write down one thing that you can do to take a step toward forgiving them. This doesn't mean that you must have a heart-to-heart with every single person who has hurt you. It could just mean that you vow today to stop gossiping about a hurtful situation. Maybe you'll commit to surrendering that relationship to the Lord. Perhaps healing can come about if you ask the Lord for the grace of empathy, to appreciate where someone is coming from. Be generous with your steps to forgiveness!

Jesus, you know so well the pain that sin causes. You endured unimaginable pain to bring about the forgiveness of my sins so that I could spend eternity in your presence. You offered your forgiveness freely to those who hurt you. Help me to surrender my feelings of pain and rejection and to place myself at the foot of the cross. Then, Lord, give me the grace to pick up my cross daily and follow your plan for me and my future marriage.

RESPONDING TO
THE LORD WITH
WILD GENEROSITY

*"This is a serious warning cry: Surrender without
reservation to the Lord who has called us. This is required
of us so that the face of the earth may be renewed."*

— Saint Edith Stein

When I was single, I sat in the local adoration chapel quite a bit.
Although I probably looked serene to the outside observer, inside my heart I was having a loud, frank conversation with the Lord. I questioned his plans for my relationships (or lack thereof), why things weren't moving along on my timeline, and how it seemed as if every friend were dating, engaged, or celebrating a wedding anniversary.

Each prayer usually ended the same way: "Lord, I'm frustrated with what my life looks like; please give me the grace to trust you." But not too much later, I would show up in the chapel again, railing and fighting against God's plan for my life.

How often we fall into the trap of telling the Lord exactly what he needs to do to make us happy!

I wish I could say that as I matured in my relationship with God, I abandoned the practice of bossing him around. But years later, I'm still patiently (well, maybe not so patiently) trying to respond to him with a generous "yes."

There are lots of things about a wedding that you can plan around and prepare for. But a lot of things are out of your control. That lack of control can be scary. In fact, it's easy to give in to the clamoring "what if's" that fill your mind, inviting you to jump to the worst-case scenario.

What if you can't decide on a place to get married?

What if no one sends an RSVP, and there's a bunch of empty tables at the reception?

What if you trip on your way down the aisle?

What if you forget something at home and the ceremony isn't quite as planned?

It's tempting and easy to let the thoughts spiral, as you clutch your plans tighter and tighter. But if you listen to the "what if's," you'll miss out on what is happening right now.

Releasing your grasp on wedding planning starts with committing to live in this season with your eyes open, ready to be generous with the Lord, others, and yourself. While it may seem backward to plan a wedding by letting go of your plans, living generously allows you to grow in your relationships, your commitment to your future vocation, and your love of God and your future spouse.

Your conscious choice to surrender your wedding day to the Lord with unashamed, wild generosity is a beautiful statement to a world that thinks God is not worthy of trust.

What does this wild generosity look like in your life as an engaged woman?

It's not just surrendering your plans for your wedding and your marriage to the Lord, although that's an important first step.

Wild generosity means total abandonment to his will, without holding anything back.

It means absolutely accepting God's plan, even if it looks completely different from what you had in mind. Wild generosity enables you to abandon the fear that God doesn't have a design for your wedding or your marriage. This generosity also helps you reject the idea that God's plan is going to disappoint you, or not quite measure up to what you had hoped for.

When you're wildly generous with the Lord, you'll be able to rejoice that the plan he has in store is bigger than you could possibly fathom.

Today, write down the "what if's" that have been tempting you to hold tight to your plan. After you've written each one down, spend time in prayer surrendering each of those specific worries to the Lord. Ask him to inspire in you a radically generous response to his plans, for your wedding day and beyond.

Heavenly Father, you have plans full of hope for my life and my marriage. Today, I want to generously give you my worries that I've been holding on to. Come into this season of my life and bring peace into these days of preparation.

_____

_____

_____

_____

_____

_____

IN THE SPOTLIGHT

*"To be taken with love for a soul, God does not look
on its greatness, but the greatness of its humility."*

— Saint John of the Cross

I t's no secret that the world loves to shine a spotlight on the bride on her wedding day. Magazines, vendors, and even friends and family sometimes forget the groom in the flurry of wedding planning.

Sometimes the spotlight gets the best of us. The pressure to have a perfect wedding day can leave the best of us struggling. It's easy to begin taking the wedding plans too seriously, push away those whom you love the most, and let stress take over.

The nature of wedding events and traditions doesn't help, either. You've probably found yourself in the center of a crowd of family and friends, unwrapping wedding gifts at your bridal shower. Friends and loved ones may have surrounded you as you tried on your wedding dress, offering compliments and advice. Maybe you've become the go-to person for all of the wedding day decisions, and you've started thinking that nothing would be ready if you weren't planning it all.

There's nothing wrong with being excited about your wedding day and sharing that excitement with those around you. But snatching the spotlight and basking in it can make it easy to forget what all of this preparation is for. The wedding day will be beautiful, but it's a day. Your friends and family are gathering to celebrate not just you, but also the shared future of you and your soon-to-be husband and your commitment to marriage before them and the Lord.

It can also be tempting to push your fiancé out of the spotlight. Wedding blogs and magazines emphasize the idea that this is "your day" as the bride, instead of "our day" as a couple approaching the sacrament of marriage together. Resist the urge to go at wedding planning heroically alone.

When Joseph and I prepared for our wedding, I had already bought into the idea that he would find wedding planning annoying and bothersome. But when we started making decisions, I discovered that Joseph had just as many hopes and desires for our wedding day (and our marriage!) as I did. Planning our wedding together and preparing for our marriage as a team helped us learn communication and collaboration skills that we're still using today, long after the flowers have wilted and the cake has been eaten.

So how can you approach this day and the attention that comes with it in a healthy way? In moments where you're tempted to stand in the artificial spotlight of wedding planning, ask yourself what your wedding day is really about. Remember to keep the desire for a healthy, holy marriage in sight, and strive to respond to the spotlight with humility.

Generous humility means asking your fiancé about the wedding planning process, and thinking of his desires before your own. Humility also means remembering who you are in relation to God — you're his daughter, and you have divine potential. But you don't have to be perfect, or buy into the spotlight in order to find your self-worth. You (and your future husband!) are made for something that burns much brighter and longer than a wedding-day spotlight. You're meant for eternity with the Lord, and your marriage should propel you to that goal ... together.

In what ways have you sought after and longed for the spotlight along this journey to the altar? Where have you given in to the temptation to gossip or stir up drama in order to sustain the attention of those surrounding you? Whose story have you failed to notice because you were too busy? Spend some time reflecting today.

Heavenly Father, it's tempting to steal the spotlight for myself in this season. When I feel the urge to put myself or my desires first, inspire me with humility and generosity. As my fiancé and I plan our wedding together, help both of us focus on the beauty and importance of our future marriage.

ARE YOU ENVIOUS?

"There is no need to worry. No one can take your seat at the table he prepares for you."

— Morgan Harper Nichols

In a parable he tells his followers, Christ describes the kingdom of heaven as a vineyard. Some workers show up at dawn to work for the vineyard owner. They agree on a fair wage and head out to the field.

Around nine in the morning, some other people show up. They've had their morning coffee, and they're ready to get at it. Again, the vineyard owner decides on a just wage with them and sends them out to work.

But there's still work to be done, and there are not enough workers in the field. So the vineyard owner ventures out at lunchtime to ask people to come to the vineyard. And at three in the afternoon, even though the sun is low in the sky, he's still inviting people.

Finally, evening falls. But the vineyard owner is still asking people to go work for him even after dinner.

At the end of the day, they all gather around the vineyard owner and put out their hands for their just wage, the wage they agreed on before setting foot in the vineyard. Then, to the shock and horror of the workers who have been laboring in the field since before breakfast, the vineyard owner gives every single worker the same paycheck.

Naturally, the first workers grumble. "This last group of workers put in less than an hour's work, and you're giving them the same benefits as us? That's not fair at all. You're cheating us. We've been here since before the sun was up!"

But the vineyard owner looks those workers in the eye, loving them. "Are you envious because I'm generous?" he asks them.

Ouch.

Sister, maybe you've been feeling lately like those workers who've been at it since the break of dawn. You're striving after God's plan for a joyful marriage. Maybe you've had this day in mind since you were a little girl. During this season of engagement, it can be easy to look around and start comparing with the lives of others. You're not alone if you struggle with this, sister. Even after marriage, I'm still wrestling with the beast of comparison.

Maybe you're still months away from your wedding day. In fact, some days it feels like it'll be years before you put on that white dress and marry your love. Even though you know you're working toward that big day, the countdown in your mind is ticking down a lot slower than you'd like. But when you log on to social media, friends are getting married left and right. That girl who got engaged after you is already settling into married life. Another friend met her soon-to-be husband way after you met your fiancé, but they're closer to their wedding day than you are.

It's tempting to flip through friends' pictures and status updates and feel envy and jealousy come crashing down on you in waves. Their honeymoon was lavish. Their photographer was better than anything you can afford. Her dress is gorgeous, and her bridesmaids look like they have it all together. You're sure your wedding cake would look like a pile of crumbs if it were side by side with hers.

All of that comparison can leave you wondering why everything seems to be coming together for everyone else while you're struggling. Maybe you're wondering why good things are happening to people who you know have stories behind those Instagram-perfect posts. You're striving for holiness, right? Shouldn't things be coming together easier?

As messy human beings, our generosity tends to be logical and limited in mercy. While the world encourages this attitude of jealousy, Christ offers a path that is so radically different it can leave us confused.

God loves generously in a way we can't comprehend. He pours out lavishly even when we don't deserve a shred of his generosity. He gives expecting nothing in return. But that lack of return on investment doesn't stop him from giving and giving!

The *Catechism of the Catholic Church* describes envy as "sadness at the sight of another's goods and the immoderate desire to have them for oneself" (2553). But being envious at the goodness God is pouring into the lives of others isn't going to help you come to the altar as a radiant bride.

Today, take time to pray and see where envy has snuck into your heart. Then, write down a time when you can go to confession and give over this spirit of envy to the Lord.

Have I found myself thinking "they deserve it" when those I know or love experience hard times?

Have I gossiped among my friends and family about someone else's story lately?

Have I changed my wedding plans in order to compete with my friends' or those I've seen on social media?

Have I been unaware of the blessings in my own life because I'm too busy looking at the gifts that God has given others?

Have I responded to the good news of others with a harsh tone, questioning why God has blessed them?

Lord, help me rejoice with those who are rejoicing. When people in my life experience joy, help me to set aside my limited, human view of generosity and instead dive head-first into your limitless generosity.

THEY HAVE NO WINE

*"At Cana, in fact, Jesus does not only recognize
the dignity and role of the feminine genius, but by
welcoming his Mother's intervention, he gives her the
opportunity to participate in his messianic work."*

— Pope Saint John Paul II

Some (okay, all) of my favorite movies are romantic comedies. I love sitting around with the women in my life over a cup of coffee and having heart-to-heart conversations about their lives and relationships. If you were to follow me on Facebook, your feed would soon be full of all the relationship articles I post. YouTube's suggestions for me include wedding videos, engagement stories, and promposals. Pinterest literally only suggests wedding items anymore — even though I'm already married!

Don't even get me started on Disney movies. Growing up, I'd spent my summers catching up on all the Disney movies that had come out over the school year. I even have a Disney soul sister: Anna from *Frozen*. I love how she jumps headfirst into love.

I can't help it … I love love.

So it wasn't a surprise when I fell in love with the story of the wedding feast at Cana, where Christ works his first public miracle in the Gospels. It has all of my favorite plot elements: a wedding day, a party, Christ, Mary, and — I'll admit it — a good glass of wine.

But what I thought was just a beautifully miraculous wedding day ended up teaching me about the Blessed Mother and her generous role in our lives.

Can you imagine inviting Christ, his mother, and his disciples to your wedding, and them showing up? Talk about wedding goals.

But then … you've spent months preparing for this party, only to run out of wine. This story could have ended many ways, but for this couple, the Blessed Mother came up to Jesus and told him, "They have no wine."

Jesus looked at his mother and responded, "O woman, what have you to do with me? My hour has not yet come." But Our Lady turned to the servants present at the wedding feast and told them, "Do whatever he tells you" (Jn 2:2–5).

No one at the party knew the full story about Jesus. He hadn't yet raised people from the dead, or given the Sermon on the Mount. But Mary knew she could trust her son to take care of things. She was so confident in entrusting the needs of the bride and groom to the Lord that she confidently told the servants to "Do whatever he tells you," even after Christ brought up the fact that his hour had not come yet.

Mary provides us with an incredible example of intentional generosity at the wedding feast at Cana. She recognizes the need of the newly married couple, and gives of her own time and attention to solve the problem. And Mary's radical generosity then inspires Christ's lavish generosity. Her generous spirit and desire to bring the needs of the newly married couple to the attention of her son encourages the Lord to perform his first public miracle.

Mary's generosity points everyone and everything back to the Lord. Yes, there is an abundance of wine at the end of the exchange between Mary and Jesus. But she also reveals that the true solution is found by turning to Christ and trusting in his generosity.

Where in your wedding story do you feel like you've run out of wine? Wherever it is that you're coming up dry in this season of engagement, follow the example of Mary at the wedding at Cana. Give your problems to the Lord, and then prepare for big things to happen. He loves lavishly, and he gives excessively.

In the space below, entrust your problem to Our Lord and the Blessed Mother. Then, be prepared to do whatever Jesus tells you to do.

Lord, it can be tempting to snatch back what I've given you. Help me to truly surrender my will and desires to your plan. Conform my will to yours, and help me trust you when I've run out of patience, generosity, or any other virtue that seems to have run dry in this season. Help me imitate Mary's radical generosity and trust as I prepare for my upcoming wedding feast, and be present there with your mother when the day comes.

_____

_____

_____

_____

_____

_____

_____

JOY PRECEDES GENEROSITY

"The point is this: he who sows sparingly will also reap
sparingly, and he who sows bountifully will also reap
bountifully. Each one must do as he has made up his mind,
not reluctantly or under compulsion, for God loves a cheerful
giver. And God is able to provide you with every blessing in
abundance, so that you may always have enough of everything
and may provide in abundance for every good work."

— 2 Corinthians 9:6–8

I'll never forget the first wedding I was in. I was singing at the wedding of a dear friend. As we waited for the wedding to start, the bridesmaids and bride settled up in the choir loft with me to wait for their cue.

I'd watched my friend grow through her engagement. We'd celebrated her bachelorette party together, and the night before, we'd stayed up late talking about what we were looking forward to the most in marriage.

But that morning, as she sat up in the choir loft, she looked at me and said, "I can't wait for this day to be over." My heart fell for her. Her wedding day, one of the most beautiful days of her life, was overshadowed by stress.

When the ceremony started, she walked down to the aisle toward her groom, smiling, and I celebrated happily with her at the reception. But I'll never forget the look in her eyes when she was up in the choir loft with me.

How do we beat the monster of wedding planning? How do we get to the point where we can confidently, joyfully walk up the aisle to our groom without worrying about the flow of the day? And how in the world can we live a life of radical generosity if we're worried about whether or not there'll be enough to go around?

Saint Teresa of Calcutta, a bride of the Lord, has the answer. "Joy is a sign of generosity," she wrote. "When you are full of joy, you move faster and you want to go about doing good to everyone."

Joy is the secret ingredient in this recipe of generosity. Think about it — have you ever met an unhappy generous person? Those who give of themselves freely inspire those around them, and remind others of the generous love of God.

Joy is authentic happiness that doesn't depend on things going right. Instead, practicing joy helps us be able to recognize the small moments in this season where God is showing up. Then, inspired by God's generosity, we can joyfully give to those around us.

But generous giving isn't only for your engagement. We're called to live this radical joy after we take those steps toward the altar, too. Catholic marriage is meant to reveal the joy and love of God to the world.

If you're feeling stressed or worried, you don't have to put on a mask of perfection. You don't have to ignore your emotions either, stuffing them down inside you because you're determined to force joy. Instead, you can take small, little steps toward joy on a daily basis.

In what ways can you incorporate joy into your life this season? What are ways (even tiny ones!) that you've already tasted the goodness of the Lord? Today, reflect on at least five ways that you've experienced joy today. Maybe you heard one of your favorite songs on the radio, or listened to the birds singing as you walked into work. Perhaps you found joy in the smell of coffee in the morning, or the fresh scent of a cool, bright, spring day. Today, instead of painting with broad brush-strokes, I challenge you to dive deep into the details of your day and find joy in the smallest ways that God has shown you his generosity.

Lord, help me be a light of joy to those around me. Help my joy, and the joy I find in my marriage after this journey to the altar, constantly point others back to you, the ultimate source of light and joy in my life. Encourage me to tune in to those seemingly insignificant, small moments and find joy in the littlest gifts you give me. Make my heart joyful and generous, so that I can approach the wedding altar overflowing with love of you.

_____

_____

_____

_____

_____

_____

_____

_____

_____

_____

_____

_____

_____

_____

_____

_____

_____

_____

_____

_____

_____

_____

_____

_____

_____

INVITING OTHERS TO
THE WEDDING FEAST

*"The soul of woman must be expansive and open to all human
beings; it must be quiet so that no small weak flame will be
extinguished by stormy winds; warm so as not to benumb fragile
buds ... empty of itself, in order that extraneous life may have
room in it; finally, mistress of itself and also of its body, so that
the entire person is readily at the disposal of every call."*

— Saint Edith Stein

When you think of generosity on your wedding day, what comes
to mind? Maybe you think of asking for charitable donations in
place of some typical wedding gift ideas. Or perhaps donating your wedding dress after the big day. But generosity on your wedding day doesn't
have to require these sorts of large gestures.

Instead, generosity on your wedding day itself simply means en-
countering others the way that Christ encounters us. He meets us in our
daily, ordinary life. He invites us to find him in the little moments of the
day, and reminds us of the grace found in the present moment.

Christ teaches us in the Gospels that he invites everyone to the wedding feast, and that's something that you and your soon-to-be spouse get to partake in for a day, too.

When Joseph and I were planning our wedding day, we decided to do something our friends and family thought was the definition of crazy. Instead of meeting with caterers to coordinate and plan our wedding meal, we decided to make the food ourselves.

We didn't make this decision because we wanted to be the ultimate wedding all-stars, or impress our guests with our (mediocre) cooking skills. Instead, we cooked our wedding dinner because we wanted to enter the wedding reception with a spirit of generosity.

It's easy to treat the wedding reception as the after-party you deserve after all of this planning and work. But Joseph and I wanted to host a dinner party to thank our friends and family for their support in our relationship. So, during the week leading up to our January wedding, we made gallons of soup in my in-laws' kitchen. We put together a salad bar and helped set everything up.

Before you start canceling your catering plans or wonder whether you're being generous even though you're having someone else make your wedding meal, don't. Making dinner for our guests was the way Joseph and I chose to live generously during our wedding week. But rest assured, it is not the only way. God invites us all to live generously, but he also invites you into a unique way of living generosity in your own life. You don't have the same story as anyone else, so the way you embrace this invitation to generous living will look completely different than the way I embraced it, or the way your sister, cousin, or best friend will live it out.

Generosity doesn't have to wait until the wedding reception, either. Maybe you have non-Catholic family and friends attending your wedding Mass. Your wedding programs themselves can offer a generous welcome to the wedding Mass by explaining why Catholics do what they do.

Just like you strive to create room in the margins during the season of engagement, you can create time in the margins of your wedding day itself, too. Take your time during the reception to visit with your guests (especially if they've traveled to your wedding!) and see how their lives are going.

Even after the wedding, there are opportunities to be generous with your guests. Don't buzz through wedding thank-you notes or see them as one last thing to do. Instead, take the time to intentionally pen each note, thanking your friends and family not only for the gifts they've given you, but also their presence on your wedding day or their support in your relationship.

Today, jot down some ideas of how you can invite others generously to your wedding feast.

Jesus, you invite all of us generously to join you at the wedding feast. Thank you for the opportunity in a small way to join your invitation. Help me to reject the world's temptation to make this day solely about myself, and instead to discern with my fiancé how to give ourselves and our time as a gift. Give me the graces of patience and generosity to interact with others that day as you interact with me as your beloved daughter.

LOVING YOUR
SOON-TO-BE SPOUSE

*"Love is never something ready made, something merely
'given' to man and woman; it is always at the same time a
'task' which they are set. Love should be seen as something
which in a sense never 'is' but is always only 'becoming,'
and what it becomes depends upon the contributions of
both persons and the depth of their commitment."*

— Pope Saint John Paul II

How often do you show generous love to your fiancé? This doesn't mean that you have to arrange lavish, intricate signs of affection. Saint Teresa of Calcutta encouraged us to do "small things with great love," and it's absolutely important that your generous heart be directed toward the love of your life.

Generous love might mean pressing pause on the wedding planning when you're together for an evening and focusing on your relationship. Maybe it's asking your love how his day was, and attentively listening to his response. Or maybe it's a quick hug and words of encouragement.

When we're busy or stressed thanks to wedding planning or other life changes, it can be easy to forget to intentionally and generously love the man we've chosen to spend the rest of our life with.

Acts of generous love and sacrifice, intentionally sprinkled throughout the day, shouldn't stop when you say "I do." There are so many different factors that go into a happy and holy marriage. Marriage preparation programs emphasize communication and how to handle conflict. But one thing that is often overlooked is the importance of simple, generous signs of affection.

This generous love will look different for each couple — after all, we all have unique stories and ways that we love being loved. But part of your mission after the altar is to convince your spouse that he is lovable and worthy of love. You are helping each other get to heaven, and your generous love can be a way for your spouse to see the Lord at work in his life.

As life continues, you'll continue to get to know your spouse even better. Throughout life surprises, new jobs, new houses, or family changes, you can always choose to give generous acts of love.

In the space below, write down a few things that you can do in the next few weeks to generously love your fiancé. Then make a plan for when you'll intentionally choose to reflect the love of Christ in his life.

Lord, you've invited me to mirror your love in the life of my fiancé. Fill me with energy and passionate enthusiasm to respond generously with a "yes" to that invitation. Encourage me to be perceptive to the way that my fiancé receives love. Inspire me to reflect your generous, selfless love not only in my engagement, but also my marriage.

Women

ACKNOWLEDGE THE PERSON

because they

SEE PERSONS

with their

HEARTS

Part Three
Sensitivity

"Perhaps more than men, women acknowledge the person, because they see persons with their hearts. They see them independently of various ideological or political systems. They see others in their greatness and limitations; they try to go out to them and help them. In this way the basic plan of the Creator takes flesh in the history of humanity and there is constantly revealed, in the variety of vocations, that beauty — not merely physical, but above all spiritual — that God bestowed from the very beginning on all, and in a particular way on women."

— Pope Saint John Paul II

YOUR SENSITIVITY
IS A STRENGTH

*"Woman naturally seeks to embrace that
which is living, personal, and whole."*

— Saint Edith Stein

When you reflect on the concept of sensitivity, what's the first thing that comes to mind?

Maybe you thought of how you were told not to wear your heart on your sleeve when you were younger. Perhaps when you think of sensitivity, you think of being irrationally overemotional, or being a fragile, deep-feeling person in a messy world. Today's culture doesn't laud sensitivity as a strength, but instead condemns it as a weakness.

If you think sensitivity makes you weak, you're not alone.

I grew up thinking that sensitivity was something to be ashamed of. When I was in grade school, I'd cry if I saw someone in pain. My nickname growing up was "compassionate Chloe," and it wasn't always said as a compliment. When I was in high school, romantic gestures in movies would move me to tears, and my friends would tease me.

I used to think that my sensitivity toward others was a character flaw. But now I realize that sensitivity is actually such an important strength in the life of women that it's an aspect of the feminine genius. More than just wearing your heart on your sleeve, sensitivity gives you the ability to see and understand the deep desires and needs of the human heart, and to respond to those desires with genuine love.

Rejecting your sensitivity would take away your ability to empathize with those around you. You'd diminish your creativity. You wouldn't be able to recognize the little things throughout the day that touch your heart. You'd be left without the passion that drives your daily decisions, and your awareness of the messy, broken hearts of others.

Sister, instead of a character flaw to overcome, your sensitivity is a gift that reveals to the world the radiant love of God.

What lies have you bought into when it comes to sensitivity? What was your understanding of sensitivity up to this point in your life? Write down your thoughts.

Next, write a letter of thanksgiving to God, thanking him for the gift of your feminine genius, especially your sensitivity. The culture (and the devil!) may have lied to you about your feminine genius before, but God calls you his beloved daughter, and he says you are good!

Lord, you've created me as your daughter. Help me to appreciate every gift that you've given me, even if our culture sees my gifts as weaknesses to be rejected. Clarify and sanctify my understanding of sensitivity so that I can better see your image reflected in the souls of those around me.

_____

_____

_____

_____

_____

_____

_____

_____

_____

_____

_____

_____

_____

_____

_____

_____

_____

_____

_____

PERFECTIONISM
IS THE OPPOSITE
OF SENSITIVITY

"Perfectionism is the belief that if we do things perfectly and look perfect, we can minimize or avoid the pain of blame, judgment, and shame. Perfectionism is a twenty-ton shield that we lug around, thinking it will protect us, when in fact it's the thing that's really preventing us from being seen."

— Brené Brown

Do you dream of a wedding day that goes off without a single hiccup? A day that is ingrained in your memory as the definition of perfection? Today, sister, I want you to let that image go.

Everything doesn't have to be perfect on the day of your wedding. In fact, everything won't be perfect.

On Joseph's and my wedding day, there were little imperfections all day long. There was a mix-up with our lectors. We forgot what we were supposed to do during part of the wedding Mass. Then, part of our wedding party showed up late to the reception.

We got married in January, and we stood outside the doors to the reception hall shivering and waiting for everyone to arrive. Greeting people as they came into the reception hadn't been the original plan. But the imperfection of our wedding schedule allowed us to see friends and family and thank them for coming.

Just as your wedding day won't be perfect, your marriage won't be perfect, either. Marriage is the joining together of two messy, broken souls who have vowed before God to journey toward his heart together, to help each other become saints.

But you'll stumble along that path. You'll fall. Your spouse will fall. Sometimes, you'll both fall together. But the beauty of marriage is that you then turn to help each other up. Limping and wounded, you'll remember your vows to love each other in good times and bad. For richer or for poorer. Until death do you part. You'll look into the eyes of your beloved and realize that this person who loves you the most is also the person whose actions will hurt you the most. In those moments — which God will offer you throughout the entirety of your journey to him — you'll have a choice.

You could choose to lock your heart away so that its sensitivity can never hurt you. But there in the darkness, your heart will grow cold. Your heart will be shut off to anything that resembles love, because you fear the way that love can leave you vulnerable to pain.

Or, you can choose to embrace your sensitivity. You can offer your heart as a refuge for your spouse, mess and all. You can offer him your whole heart, even with the knowledge that sometimes he will break it.

Today, reject the lure of perfectionism for both your wedding day and for your marriage. A friend told me once that perfectionism is the opposite of sensitivity. Instead of being aware of our hearts and the hearts of others, perfectionism urges us to push away the messiness of other people's stories.

In the space below, ask God for the grace to willingly accept his plan for your marriage. Surrender your wedding day to his love. Open your clenched fists that hold on to your plans for perfection.

Father, the world encourages me to chase after the perfect wedding day and the perfect marriage. But I know that my wedding day and my marriage will be filled with the stories and flaws of messy hearts — mine included. Give me the grace to trust you not only with our wedding day, but also with the rest of my life. Leave no stone unturned in my heart as you draw me closer to your sacred heart.

AVOIDING OVERSENSITIVITY

*"I therefore, a prisoner for the Lord, beg you to walk
in a manner worthy of the calling to which you have
been called, with all lowliness and meekness, with
patience, forbearing one another in love, eager to
maintain the unity of the Spirit in the bond of peace."*

— Ephesians 4:1–3

Sensitivity can play a beautiful role in our lives as women. With it, we can be sensitive to the effects of sin. Sensitivity can open us to an awareness of the suffering hearts of others, and strengthen us to offer help. Christ invites us to foster sensitivity to the Holy Spirit so that we can respond to his inspirations as we pursue a life of holiness.

But oversensitivity, in the sense of emotional overreaction, especially during an already emotional time of change, can actually hinder our feminine genius. Oversensitivity can cause small wounds to seem much worse, and any suffering can be much more destructive.

Pope Saint John Paul II knew about the delicate line between embracing authentic sensitivity and becoming overly sensitive. "The woman of course, as much as the man, must take care that her sensitivity does not succumb to the temptation to possessive selfishness, and must put it at the service of authentic love," he said to a crowd gathered to pray the Angelus in the summer of 1995. "On these conditions she gives of her best, everywhere adding a touch of generosity, tenderness, and joy of life."

Have you struggled with oversensitivity on your way to the altar? Maybe friends and family haven't reacted to news about your upcoming wedding day with the joy you had hoped they would, or you've been taking the "no" responses on RSVPs personally. Perhaps the decor you'd planned to DIY has crumbled around you, leaving you scrambling and wondering whether the entire day will fall apart like your centerpieces. Or maybe what should have been a little disagreement with your future groom exploded into a big fight.

If it seems like you've been on an emotional roller coaster in the past few months, you're not alone. Most brides can point to one or two times during their wedding preparation when a small issue was blown out of proportion.

How can you combat the temptation to oversensitivity? First, remember that sensitivity isn't a vice that we have to put to death in our lives. If you're struggling with oversensitivity in this season, it's not the sensitivity that has to go. It's the selfishness.

If you find yourself becoming personally offended even when little things go wrong, it may be because you've placed yourself at the center of this season. When you buy into an all-about-me mentality, it's easy to fall into the trap of oversensitivity.

Everything that is done (or forgotten!), along with everyone's motives and intentions, can be misconstrued as a reflection on you. Oh, sister, that is a heavy load to carry by yourself.

Today, take a step away from the center. Pray for the grace of selflessness. That RSVP from a family friend who can't make it to the wedding more than likely isn't about you, it's about something they're going through or need to do. The centerpieces that look pieced together aren't a reflection of who you are as a daughter of God.

If you find yourself struggling with oversensitivity, humility is a beautiful virtue to work on fostering in this season.

Humility is perhaps the most misunderstood virtue there is. Practicing humility doesn't mean thinking that you're worthless, or too small to notice. Instead, it's recognizing who you are in relation to the Lord.

Yes, we're in great need of his help when it comes to our journey to the altar, and throughout our entire life. But he's also created us with divine potential. With the virtue of humility, you'll be able to look at yourself through the eyes of a loving Father — and his gaze can set you free.

When Joseph and I were preparing for our wedding, I found myself praying the Litany of Humility to help me combat my desire to be in the center of things:

> *O Jesus! Meek and humble of heart, hear me.*
> *From the desire of being esteemed, deliver me, Jesus.*
> *From the desire of being loved …*
> *From the desire of being extolled …*
> *From the desire of being honored …*
> *From the desire of being praised …*
> *From the desire of being preferred to others …*
> *From the desire of being consulted …*
> *From the desire of being approved …*
> *From the fear of being humiliated …*
> *From the fear of being despised …*
> *From the fear of suffering rebukes …*
> *From the fear of being calumniated …*
> *From the fear of being forgotten …*
> *From the fear of being ridiculed …*
> *From the fear of being wronged …*
> *From the fear of being suspected …*
>
> *That others may be loved more than I, Jesus, grant me the grace to desire it.*
> *That others may be esteemed more than I …*

That, in the opinion of the world, others may increase
and I may decrease ...
That others may be chosen and I set aside ...
That others may be praised and I unnoticed ...
That others may be preferred to me in everything ...
That others may become holier than I, provided that I
may become as holy as I should ...

Striving for humility doesn't mean that you should think less of yourself, or spend time combating oversensitivity with self-deprecation. Instead, it simply means thinking of yourself less and others more, and backing away from the center of attention.

Which words from the Litany of Humility most struck your heart? Copy them out, then spend time journaling about those particular phrases. Once you've spent time with a phrase, relate your thoughts to the Lord. Spend time in prayer telling him what you're thinking and feeling. Then receive what the Lord wants to communicate to you through this phrase.

Finally, make a resolution based on your prayer. What will you do next when the temptation to react in an oversensitive way arises? Ask the Lord to help you foster humility in your heart and in your daily life.

Lord, it's tempting during this season to see any little problem or personal slight as a reflection of who I am. Instead of falling victim to the whims of the day's goings-on, help me to find stability in you as my foundation. Remind me that I'm your beloved daughter, regardless of who shows up at the wedding, the decorations on the tables, or any other detail that I'm allowing to wound me deeper than it should. Give me clarity of heart and mind.

FOSTERING SENSITIVITY TOWARD THE HEART OF CHRIST

"Mary would rather have had all His sufferings herself, could that have been, than not have known what they were by ceasing to be near Him. He, too, gained a refreshment, as from some soothing and grateful breath of air, to see her sad smile amid the sights and the noises which were about Him. She had known Him beautiful and glorious, with the freshness of Divine Innocence and peace upon His countenance; now she saw Him so changed and deformed that she could scarce have recognized Him, save for the piercing, thrilling, peace-inspiring look He gave her."

— Blessed John Henry Newman

From his first breath on this earth until his last breath on the cross, Christ was accompanied by women who saw and understood his mission and responded to him with genuine and sacrificial love.

Our Lady birthed and raised Jesus, accompanying him during

those silent years before his public ministry. Then, when Christ began his mission here on earth, Mary Magdalene, Joanna, and Susanna all accompanied and supported him. Christ visited the house of Mary and Martha, and rested with them.

During Christ's passion and death, it was Veronica who broke through the crowds and wiped the face of Jesus with her veil. The women of Jerusalem met him along the road and mourned with him. The Blessed Mother stood at the foot of the cross, never abandoning her son and Savior.

Then, it was women who followed Christ's body to the tomb, returning with spices and perfumed oils to prepare him for burial.

It only seems fitting that these women, who witnessed the intimate suffering of the Lord, were the first witnesses to his glorious resurrection.

"The women are the first at the tomb. They are the first to find it empty. They are the first to hear: 'He is not here, He has risen, as he said.' They are the first to embrace his feet. They are also the first to be called to announce the truth to the Apostles," Pope Saint John Paul II wrote in his apostolic letter *Mulieris Dignitatem*.

But women's sensitivity toward the heart and mission of Christ didn't stop after his resurrection or ascension into heaven.

In fact, Christ still calls us today, in this very moment, to console his heart especially with our feminine gifts. It seems an ironic task, if not impossible. How are we, the created, to console the heart of the Creator himself? Isn't Christ perfectly happy in heaven? If so, surely he doesn't need our sensitivity.

Even though Christ's crucifixion was a real, historic event that happened at a designated point in history, the Lord exists outside of time. Christ suffered for all the sins committed throughout human history. Because of this, he felt the weight of the ways that we hurt his heart, thousands of years after he walked to this earth.

So, just as we can add to the weight of Christ's suffering with our sins, we can also alleviate some of Christ's suffering and console his heart.

We can sit with him in his pain, seeing and feeling his suffering with our own hearts. Our unique feminine sensitivity can draw us closer to the heart of Christ.

"It's not so hard to imagine Jesus full of sorrow in the Garden of Gethsemane, because he could somehow foresee the rejection, betrayal, and apostasy of future generations," writes Father Michael Gaitley in *Consoling the Heart of Jesus*. "At the same time, it's not so hard to imagine Jesus, during that same agony in the garden, being consoled by his awareness of the many people in the future who would love and follow him."

Christ's suffering is a mystery to us, and one we won't be able to fully understand while here on earth. Jesus doesn't physically suffer continuously from the pain of crucifixion. After all, he rose from the tomb!

But according to mystics such as Saint Faustina and Saint Thérèse of Lisieux, Christ's heart does suffer because of our sin, and he asks us to console him.

"My daughter, know that if I allow you to feel and have a more profound knowledge of My sufferings, that is a grace from Me," Christ told Saint Faustina after she experienced intense physical pain. "But when your mind is dimmed and your sufferings are great, it is then that you take an active part in My passion, and I am conforming you more fully to Myself. It is your task to submit yourself to My will at such times, more than at others" (*Diary*, 1697).

Beautifully, this season of engagement can be a time when you can intentionally console the Lord's heart as you prepare to encounter him in the Sacrament of Marriage.

Instead of giving in to countless distractions, take time to attune your heart to the heart of the Lord. He knows what it is like to be in a season of preparation, a season that stretches. Consoling his heart doesn't mean lavish gestures, but simply existing with the Lord and being present with him.

While you prepare your heart to meet your beloved at the altar, make a plan for peace in a season of busyness to intentionally console the heart of Christ. Schedule a time this week for confession and prayer. Encounter the Lord's justice, mercy, and love.

Then make a concrete plan to sit with the Lord as you prepare for a sacrament that allows you to mirror the radical love he showed on the cross. Pencil in time to console the Lord's heart, and pray and meditate on the following prayer of Saint Faustina.

I want to love you as no human soul has ever loved you before; and although I am utterly miserable and small, I have, nevertheless, cast the anchor of my trust deep down into the abyss of your mercy.

_____

_____

_____

_____

_____

_____

_____

_____

_____

_____

_____

MARY AND ELIZABETH

*"The hour is coming, in fact has come, when the vocation
of woman is being achieved in its fullness, the hour in
which woman acquires in the world an influence, an effect
and a power never hitherto achieved. That is why, at this
moment when the human race is under-going so deep a
transformation, women impregnated with the spirit of the
Gospel can do so much to aid mankind in not falling."*

— Pope Saint Paul VI

Friendships between women can get a bad rap. Women are often
stereotyped as jealous, catty, and judgmental, and friendships with
women portrayed as complicated and messy.

But we don't have to live in a Mean Girls world. Feminine friendships offer incredible opportunity for spiritual growth and community.
Instead of buying into the world's expectations, we can find the perfect
example of feminine, sensitive friendship in the Blessed Virgin Mary.

Can you imagine being in Mary's shoes? The angel Gabriel appeared to her and told her that, despite her virginity, she was going
to be the mother of the Savior of the world. But instead of getting a

moment to process this huge, life-altering announcement, Mary was instead asked to go visit her cousin Elizabeth, a woman who was once called barren but, through a chain of miraculous events, was expecting a baby, too.

Many women would have done a double take, myself included. If I was just informed by an angel that I'm pregnant with God, I probably wouldn't have been incredibly excited about a road trip. The Lord wasn't asking Mary to just take a quick jog down the road. Tradition tells us that Elizabeth and Zechariah probably lived in or near the city of Hebron, which was nearly a one-hundred-mile trip from Nazareth. So it would have taken Mary about a week or longer to make the journey on foot.

Yet Mary wasn't angry or jealous over Elizabeth's pregnancy. Granted, it helped that she was immaculately conceived and didn't struggle with sin. If I had been in her place, jealousy would have crept into my heart. God has just been conceived in my womb, yet I was being asked to go celebrate Elizabeth's miraculous pregnancy?

But Mary didn't go to visit Elizabeth out of curiosity or to see whether the angel Gabriel was telling her the truth. Instead, she humbly went to help her cousin through her pregnancy, sensitive to the challenges that she might be facing, and to celebrate her blessings.

Beautifully, Mary is rewarded for her generous acceptance of God's will. When she reaches the end of her trip, Elizabeth greets her with humility, beautifully pausing to rejoice in Mary's new role as the Mother of God. Mary, who had made the journey with a mission to serve, found herself praised and blessed.

If you've struggled in the past to form friendships with other women, Mary offers us an incredible example. As women, we have to take this Marian example and live it out in our own lives, embracing intentional friendships. Mary's friendship with Elizabeth encourages us to develop strong spiritual friendships, encounters that go beyond the surface level and don't shy away from deep, meaningful conversation.

These two women's intimate shared prayer inspires us to share in prayerful friendship with the women in our lives. The Visitation shows us the beauty that blooms from prayer and service to others.

Mary was receptive to God's will, and through her "yes" to his plan, she was able to physically bring Christ into Elizabeth's life and even begin a new friendship between their sons. In your own life as an engaged woman, how is the Lord inviting you to be a channel through which he can encounter others?

Use the space below to reflect on your relationships with friends and family during this season of your life. Is there any person in particular to whom Christ is inviting you to be sensitive?

Father, you inspired the Blessed Mother to go with haste to the hill country and visit Elizabeth. Encourage the gift of sensitivity in my own story, so that I can encounter others in my life with the genuine connection and love that Mary extended to Elizabeth. Reveal to me the relationships you desire me to invest in and the particular ways that I can bring the light of your life into the stories of those around me.

_____

_____

_____

_____

_____

_____

_____

LOVING SOMEONE WHO IS BROKEN

"Behold, I am doing a new thing; now it springs forth, do you not perceive it? I will make a way in the wilderness and rivers in the desert."

— Isaiah 43:19

A lmost all of us have done it. Perhaps it was after a hard breakup, a long time spent daydreaming, or a genuine hope to prepare for the future, but most of us at one point or another wrote down "the list," sketching out what we hoped, dreamed, and prayed our future spouse would be like.

I grew up dreaming of the guy I would marry. He'd have a good sense of humor, love Jesus, and preferably be taller than I was in my favorite pair of boots.

When I met my now-husband, he made me laugh. His love for his faith was infectious. He was only a few inches taller than I am when I have no shoes on at all. The more I got to know him, the more I realized he was better than any man I'd imagined in middle school, or journaled about in high school.

But despite friends telling us that we were perfect together, that he was my perfect match, or that we made a perfect couple, it didn't take me long to realize that he was far from perfect. So was I.

The more I got to know him, the more I realized that both of our stories were full of imperfections, flaws, and mistakes we regretted. He was gritty, raw, messy, and broken. His brokenness broke my heart, and my messiness broke his.

As we continued to discern marriage, we trusted each other with the truth of our stories. I dismantled my mistaken dreams of the "perfect" relationship; and together, we took the pieces of our hearts and brought them to our God. We put ourselves, all of our selves, at the feet of the God who hung, broken on the cross, the God who daily, hourly, breaks himself open in the Eucharistic feast, giving us his very body. His sacred heart, wounded by our brokenness, provided a place of healing. God's perfection and beauty encouraged both of us, imperfect and flawed, to strive for wholeness.

"Broken things are precious," Archbishop Fulton J. Sheen wrote. "We eat broken bread because we share in the depth of our Lord and His broken life. Broken flowers give perfume. Broken incense is used in adoration. A broken ship saved Paul and many other passengers on their way to Rome. Sometimes the only way the good Lord can get into some hearts is to break them."

Today, invite Jesus to bring hope and resurrection to areas of your life, your relationship, or your wedding planning that are damaged and bruised. Rest your head on his pierced heart. Ask the Lord to bless your brokenness, and let him transform it into a blessing.

Jesus, on the cross you opened yourself up to all of our brokenness. Stretched on the wood of those beams, you experienced all of the pain caused by our sins. When I'm hurt by the ones I love the most, help me run to you and embrace the cross. Your radical love on the cross opened the gates of heaven for us here. May your brokenness

help heal my brokenness, and inspire me to love the broken souls who are closest to me.

_____

_____

_____

_____

_____

_____

_____

_____

_____

_____

_____

_____

_____

FORGIVING YOURSELF

"When suddenly you seem to lose all you thought you had gained, do not despair. Your healing is not a straight line. You must expect setbacks and regressions. Don't say to yourself 'All is lost. I have to start all over again.' This is not true. What you have gained, you have gained. ... When you return to the road, you return to the place where you left it, not where you started."

— Henri J. M. Nouwen

You're running late to that meeting ... again. For some reason, you can't seem to stop making snide remarks to those you love the most. Maybe you're questioning all of your wedding plan decisions, and the stress surrounding the day is straining your relationships. We all make mistakes, from spilled coffee all over the kitchen floor to words misspoken in moments of anger or frustration. Maybe you're frustrated about how you're not making as much progress as you'd hoped in overcoming sin or building up your relationship with your future spouse.

After moments like these, it's easy to fall into the trap of self deprecation. Our inner critic rears her ugly head, reminding us of all the ways we've messed up. It's not too hard to convince ourselves that we're never going to get anything right, and surely no one else struggles like this.

Every single one of us has messy parts in our lives, and ugly moments we wish hadn't happened. Some of us may look back on our journey to the altar and see compromises, places we've let down ourselves, God, and those we love. But regardless of any mistakes you've made, your story is worthy of self-compassion instead of constant inner criticism.

"We are not the sum of our weaknesses and failures," Pope Saint John Paul II said in a homily at the seventeenth World Youth Day. "We are the sum of the Father's love for us and our real capacity to become the image of his Son."

Sensitivity allows us to see and understand the desires of the human heart, and to respond to those desires with the gaze and action of love. Yet sometimes we find ourselves able to make allowances for and forgive everyone else's mistakes but our own.

Today, take time to reflect on something you've struggled to forgive yourself for. If you haven't taken this weight to the Sacrament of Confession yet, make time this week to encounter Christ's genuine forgiveness.

Lord, today I come to you asking for the grace of forgiveness. I don't want to define myself by my weakness, or shut myself off from healing. Transform my negative and abusive thoughts about myself and inspire me to see and accept how marvelously you've created me. Help me to realize that my mistakes are never too much for your love.

APPRECIATING YOUR OWN STORY

"Thank you, every woman, for the simple fact of being a woman! Through the insight which is so much a part of your womanhood you enrich the world's understanding and help to make human relations more honest and authentic."

— Pope Saint John Paul II

What comes to your mind when you think of the wedding day of a Catholic woman who's living out the feminine genius?

I first learned about the feminine genius when I was engaged, but I worried that I wouldn't make the cut. I didn't even fit into society's beauty standards, let alone what I thought were the Catholic Church's standards for women.

After all, I was (and still am!) the woman who had to confess cursing in the confessional more than I liked.

I struggled to pray the Rosary. I had a bad case of impatience, and during the wedding planning process, I struggled with communication.

I found myself flipping through bridal magazines, browsing Pinterest, and clicking through wedding blogs, looking for inspiration. I bought into the lies of perfectionism and constantly had to stop myself from falling into the trap of comparison.

But I was thinking about the feminine genius all wrong. The feminine genius isn't a box you have to stuff yourself into. It's not a cookie-cutter model for how to live authentically as a Catholic woman. There is no one, right way to live the feminine genius on your way to the altar, or in your marriage. In fact, it will look different in the life of every woman, because we each have our own story.

In his "Letter to Women," Pope Saint John Paul II thanked women for their contributions to the world. He thanked women who are wives, daughters, and sisters. He thanked women who work, who influence the culture, and who are consecrated. Get this — he actually finished by thanking every woman for the simple fact of being a woman.

"It is thus my hope, dear sisters, that you will reflect carefully on what it means to speak of the 'genius of women,' not only in order to be able to see in this phrase a specific part of God's plan which needs to be accepted and appreciated, but also in order to let this genius be more fully expressed in the life of society as a whole, as well as in the life of the Church," Pope Saint John Paul II wrote.

Living as authentic Catholic women requires sensitivity toward our own story. We have to be aware of who we are, our deep desires and heart-level needs.

Don't chase after someone else's vision. Instead, strive for authenticity in all aspects of your life. Regardless of your personality type, your background, your virtues and vices, Christ invites you to live out the feminine genius in your own radically unique way.

If there is one thing to know about the feminine genius, it's that it is an invitation to live a life of loving, radical freedom, not a life of constriction. How do you uniquely live out the feminine genius in your daily life as a Catholic woman on her way to the altar? Take time to reflect on the question.

Lord, you've created me as good. In a season of life where the world encourages me to conform to standards of beauty and a day of perfection, help me instead rejoice as the unique, beautiful daughter that you've created me to be. Help me be sensitive to the way you've made me live out the feminine genius, especially during this time of transition, and to not be afraid to live authentically.

_____

_____

_____

_____

_____

_____

_____

_____

_____

_____

CELEBRATING THOSE WHO ARE SENSITIVE TO YOUR STORY

*"When we honestly ask ourselves which person in our lives
mean the most to us, we often find that it is those who,
instead of giving advice, solutions, or cures, have chosen
rather to share our pain and touch our wounds with a
warm and tender hand. The friend who can be silent with
us in a moment of despair or confusion, who can stay with
us in an hour of grief and bereavement, who can tolerate
not knowing, not curing, not healing and face with us the
reality of our powerlessness, that is a friend who cares."*

— Henri J. M. Nouwen

Your journey to the altar didn't start with a proposal and a ring. It
doesn't even find its origins in the years before that first date with
the man you'll soon be calling your husband.

No, yours is a story that God has had in mind since the beginning of time.

Scripture says that the Father knew you even before he formed you in your mother's womb. Before you were born, he dedicated you. Since the beginning of time, he has had a purpose for every part of your story.

He's a divine storyteller, and he delights in your story.

But this isn't a journey to the altar that you've walked alone. You're traveling on a path to the Lord's heart, and he's given you people to journey with you along that path.

Maybe your family has been beside you through your best and your worst. They've seen you raw, gritty, and growing. Perhaps you've been blessed with memories of authentic friendship that have pushed you to become the woman you are today. Maybe another couple has mentored and guided you and your fiancé during your season of discernment.

Your journey to the altar is unique and beautiful, and the support and community you'll be surrounded with on the day of your wedding is also unique to your story.

In a season where it's tempting to focus on yourself and the list of things that must be completed before the big day, take time today to be grateful for the support and relationships the Lord blesses you with.

Is there someone in your life who is happy to see you every time you spend time with them? Are the arms of your dearest friend always open, welcoming you after a long day? Does a friend keep reaching out to connect with you, despite the busyness of this season? Today, give thanks for these people's sensitivity toward your heart and your story.

Lord, thank you for the incredible witnesses to hope and joy that you've placed in my life. Today I especially think of those who have come along beside me in moments of intense pain and incredible joy. In those moments, these dear ones mirrored your divine love in my life. Help me

never to take these friendships and relationships for granted, and to always appreciate those who truly see me and reflect your steady friendship.

NURTURING
SENSITIVITY TO BEAUTY

"When Beauty fires the Blood, how Love exalts the Mind."

— John Dryden

I had dreamed about my wedding dress for years before I wore an engagement ring. So during my season of engagement, I couldn't wait to encounter the beauty of wedding gowns. I eagerly searched through wedding magazines and Pinterest boards, looking for inspiration.

But after scrolling past hundreds of wedding dresses online and turning through racks and racks of gorgeous white gowns in bridal stores, I was exhausted. All of the wedding dresses started to look the same.

At the end of the day, the lace, chiffon, silk, and organza muddled together into a single, uninspiring white blur. I looked through so many dresses that I couldn't recognize the beauty in any of them.

"Overindulgence blunts sensitivity to beauty, just as overexposure to the sun dims our vision," writes John-Mark L. Miravalle in *Beauty: What It Is and Why It Matters.*

I found myself overwhelmed. The search for a wedding dress had become just another task to tackle on time, instead of a chance to encounter and appreciate beauty.

So many aspects of wedding planning are filled to the brim with beauty — detailed dresses, vivid music, elegant stationary, vibrant flowers, and delicate calligraphy, just to name a few. Pinterest boards, bridal magazines, friends' weddings, and all forms of social media beckon to brides, offering countless examples of beauty.

But inspiration can transform into indifference. "[T]oo much sensory stimulation can blind you to the deeper realities latent in sensible realties," Miravalle notes. How can you, as a bride-to-be, nurture a sensitivity to the beauty that surrounds your upcoming wedding day?

Begin by remembering that beauty is a window here on earth through which you can encounter the Creator. Beauty on earth reveals small glimpses of the ultimate beauty awaiting us in heaven. Beaded details and blossoming bouquets are all meant to direct your heart, soul, and mind back to the Lord.

Your wedding dress may end up sitting cleaned and pressed in a coat closet. The bouquet will eventually dry out. But the Lord's beauty? It's an unending, ever-abundant well.

If you find yourself overstimulated by the choices you must make before the wedding day, turn to the words of the Psalmist:

One thing have I asked of the Lord,
    that will I seek after;
that I may dwell in the house of the Lord
    all the days of my life,
to behold the beauty of the Lord,
    and to inquire in his temple.
                        — Psalm 27:4

There's nothing wrong with a desire for your wedding day to be beautiful. But this pursuit of beauty is of no avail unless you first take time to abide with Beauty himself.

Today, copy the words from the psalm in the space below. Ask Jesus to show you the face of the Father, the face of beauty. Then take time to reflect on any areas of this season of engagement in which you've become indifferent to beauty, and ask the Lord to open your eyes to where you can encounter him in that area.

Lord, you create beauty, and you are beauty itself. Fill me with the desire to encounter you in the beauty of this season. Let every decision I make with my future spouse about our wedding day be a constant invitation to encounter you, author of beauty. Fill this season of my life with your radiance, God.

_____

_____

_____

_____

_____

_____

_____

_____

_____

_____

IN conceiving
AND giving birth
TO A CHILD
the WOMan
DISCOVERS HERSELF
through a Sincere
GIFT OF SELF

Part Four
Maternity

"A woman by her very nature is maternal — for every woman, whether married or unmarried, is called upon to be a biological, psychological or spiritual mother — she knows intuitively that to give, to nurture, to care for others, to suffer with and for them — for maternity implies suffering — is infinitely more valuable in God's sight than to conquer nations and fly to the moon."

— Dr. Alice Von Hildebrand

THE MOTHER WOUND

"In dangers, in doubts, in difficulties, think of Mary, call upon Mary. Let not her name depart from your lips, never suffer it to leave your heart. And that you may obtain the assistance of her prayer, neglect not to walk in her footsteps."

— Saint Bernard of Clairvaux

When you reflect on your childhood, you may be blessed with happy and beautiful memories of your mother. But some may be haunted by memories of their mother that involve brokenness, messiness, miscommunication, and heartbreak. Many of our stories are scarred with wounds from where our mothers unintentionally or intentionally hurt us.

As you enter into the vocation of marriage, this is a beautiful season of life in which to ponder your own motherhood, whether that ultimately means a biological or spiritual maternity. But as you discover your unique call to motherhood, thoughts and memories of your relationship with your mother will arise.

Maybe your relationship with your mother is healthy and wholesome, a gift to be thankful for. But every single mother here on this earth is human. Every mother has made mistakes. Whether your mother has hurt you in big ways or small ways, there is one mother in all of our lives who won't let us down.

Each one of us, regardless of our history with our biological mother, can find a mother in Our Lady. Mary is the mother whom Christ gave every single one of us from the cross.

"Jesus wants you to accept his mother as your own and to develop a deepening relationship with her so that she can fill the void that the past has left inside of you. And in her kind, motherly way, she will. What's more, she will lead you to her son, who as God, is the ultimate source of healing and peace," writes Marge Steinhage Fenelon in her book *Forgiving Mother.*

During this season of discerning your own maternity, ask the Blessed Mother to guide you. She isn't going to coerce or pressure her way into your life, but instead waits for your simple invitation.

But at the moment you ask her, she'll be by your side and won't ever leave you.

Healing mother wounds takes time, and sometimes the process of healing can seem like it will take a lifetime. Yet despite its arduousness, this is not an impossible task, and you are not alone.

You have a mother who only desires your good, whose only wish is to lead you to the heart of her Son, Jesus.

Copy out the words of Saint Teresa of Calcutta, "Mary, Mother of Jesus, please be a mother to me now." Then, consecrate this season of wedding planning, as well as your process of healing from mother wounds, to Our Lady. Write out exactly what you would like to place in her hands, then trust that she will walk alongside you during this season.

My queen, my mother, I give myself entirely to you. And to show my devotion to you, I consecrate to you this day, my eyes, my ears, my mouth, my heart, my entire self without reserve. As I am your own, my good mother, guard me and defend me as your property and possession. Amen. (composed by Nicolaus Zucchi)

SPIRITUAL MATERNITY

*"A woman's vocation to motherhood emanates in all
her relationships, whether she is a mother physically,
spiritually, or both. The mystery and beauty of a woman
is unequivocally tied to the fact that she bears life."*

— Alejandra M. Correa

Who comes to mind when you think of the mothers in your life?
I first think of my own mom, who fostered my love of reading
and writing. My grandma taught me to play piano and sew a dress. My
friend's mom had the cool snacks, and sometimes let us stay up past our
bedtime during sleepovers. The women at the church I attended during
college always make sure to say hello when I'm back in town. In my life
today, religious sisters are showing me what it means to love Jesus with
my whole heart.

While some of these women are called "mom" by their own physical
children, other women in my life who taught me the depth and beauty
of motherhood have never given birth. While I love thinking back on
examples of spiritual mothers in my life, when it comes to my own story,
sometimes spiritual motherhood can feel like a consolation prize.

Your journey to the altar will not go exactly as you planned, and your journey to motherhood may take unexpected twists and turns, too.

You may come to know the pains of a motherhood that doesn't quite look like what you anticipated. The Lord may invite you to parent a saint, calling littles to heaven before you can watch them grow up. You and your husband may experience the struggle of infertility.

If any of these situations are close to your heart, you may feel as if the call to spiritual maternity is a second-rate motherhood. But that couldn't be further from the truth.

In one of my favorite pieces of writing from Pope Saint John Paul II's papacy, "Letter to Women," he writes that spiritual motherhood has "inestimable value for the development of individuals and the future of society." He also thanks women for their generosity, their willingness to give themselves to others — especially the most weak and defenseless.

Maternity is an incredible calling from the Father. Regardless of what your future family looks like, the world needs your motherhood, sister. Just like you will live out the feminine genius in your unique way, spiritual motherhood looks different in the life of every woman.

"In the life of consecrated women, for example, who live according to the charism and the rules of the various apostolic Institutes, it can express itself as concern for people, especially the most needy: the sick, the handicapped, the abandoned, orphans, the elderly, children, young people, the imprisoned and, in general, people on the edges of society," Pope Saint John Paul II wrote in his apostolic letter *Mulieris Dignitatem*.

Motherhood is built into every woman, regardless of her state in life. This spiritual maternity is a universal call for women who are engaged, married, or called to religious life. It's a call for women whose children are grown and out of the house, and women who have never grown children in their womb. It's a call for women who adopt children, struggle with infertility, or suffer under the weight of miscarriage.

"Perhaps instead of saying every woman is a mother (though I believe it is true), we might say every woman is called to mother. Mother is a verb. And it's what we do," writes Danielle Bean.

This mothering comes in many unique forms. The woman who

recognizes the smallest needs of others is a mother. The woman who prays for others and cherishes them like her own daughters and sons is a mother. The woman who walks alongside someone in her life during a time of hardship is a mother.

Perhaps the Lord wants to transform the cross you're carrying into a bridge to his heart for others in your life. What areas of your life are an invitation for you to dive deeper into spiritual maternity? Take time to reflect on how you can live out spiritual maternity not only as an engaged woman, but also in your future as a married woman, too.

Lord, help me realize that I am called to mirror your love to the weak and defenseless in my life. Help me recognize that this isn't confined to physical motherhood, but that I'm called to spiritual maternity as well. Help me nurture growth in the lives of others, defend those who are in need, and make the world a better place that reflects your love.

_____

_____

_____

_____

_____

_____

DISCERNING PHYSICAL MOTHERHOOD

"The Most Important Person on earth is a mother. She cannot claim the honor of having built Notre Dame Cathedral. She need not. She has built something more magnificent than any cathedral — a dwelling for an immortal soul, the tiny perfection of her baby's body. The angels have not been blessed with such a grace. They cannot share in God's creative miracle to bring new saints to Heaven. Only a human mother can. Mothers are closer to God the Creator than any other creature; God joins forces with mothers in performing this act of creation. ... What on God's good earth is more glorious than this; to be a mother?"

— Venerable Cardinal Joseph Mindszenty

After you say "I do," it's easy to assume that the season of discernment is over. After all, you've discerned God's call for your life, made a big decision, and are ready to settle into married life! But discernment with your spouse is just getting started.

Too often, we restrict discernment to the vocational level. We're used to being asked how we discerned marriage with our fiancé, and perhaps we have watched friends and family around us discern vocations to the religious life or priesthood. But every time you and your future spouse are faced with a life-impacting decision, you're called to discern with each other and with God.

In marriage, you'll think and pray through job decisions, housing decisions, and a multitude of other situations. At some point, you'll have to discern when to add a little soul to your family.

Discerning children can be tough — especially when your story includes infertility, tough financial situations, or loss. There may be seasons in which you desire to add a baby to your family, but circumstances stand in the way.

But you're not left without resources. Practically, the Church offers Natural Family Planning as a way for spouses to not only discern how and when to add children to their family, but also as a way to grow closer to one another and in appreciation of the goodness of each other's bodies.

"These methods respect the bodies of the spouses, encourage tenderness between them, and favor the education of an authentic freedom," the *Catechism* reads (157).

Regardless of how you discern to add children to your family, whether that's through physical, biological parenthood; foster care; adoption; or spiritual parenting, invite Christ into those conversations (even right now, in your season of engagement). Here are three prayers that dear friends of ours taught us when Joseph and I were discerning our family. You can pray them with your future spouse when discerning parenthood.

"Lord, help us to desire children in the way that you desire children for our family."

God has a plan for your family. It won't always line up with your plan. Some parts of your journey will include things you did not choose and wish you could change. But God allows all of these experiences in your lives for a purpose.

Maybe you and your fiancé have no problem sharing with each other what you both desire. As you listen to each other's hopes and dreams, take time to turn to God and listen in prayer to his plans for your future family.

Surrender your plans to the Lord and ask him to make your heart burn with his desires for your family. This doesn't mean that your hearts will automatically ignite with a wildfire of clear desires — although he may answer your prayer in this way! But also prepare for the Lord to slowly fan the flames of your hearts so that you can be on the same page with each other and with his will.

"Lord, unite us in this discernment."

Discerning something with the man you love shouldn't be an experience that divides you as a couple.

If conversations together about your future family leave you frustrated, it's tempting to pray that your future spouse would just get on the same page as you. Maybe you're passionate about adoption, but your fiancé is hesitant. Maybe you're comfortable with a certain number of children, but your future spouse has something different in mind.

Praying that God will change your husband-to-be's mind won't unite you as a couple, though. Instead, pray that God will make you of one heart and mind in this discernment. Pray to be able to say "no" or "yes" to opportunities together and make decisions as a team.

"Lord, help us abide with contentment in this season of discernment."

"Abide in me, and I in you. As the branch cannot bear fruit by itself, unless it abides in the vine, neither can you, unless you abide in me," Christ says in John 15:4. Christ encourages you to abide with him in every season of your life. After all, apart from his grace, we can do nothing. But if you choose to abide in him, your marriage will bear fruit.

The fruit of your future marriage may not look like the fruit you expected. Maybe you'll add children to your family right away. Maybe years will pass before children are in the picture for you and your future spouse. Regardless of your fertility, the number of littles God will bless you with here or in heaven, or wherever you're at in the discernment process of bringing new life into your family, he invites you to abide in him.

Be content to wait at his feet, soaking up his goodness. Learn to love him for who he is, not just for the gifts he gives. And there, in that abiding, you'll encounter a God who desires to make your marriage fruitful in the most perfect way for you as a couple and as a family.

Which of these three prayers do you think will be the most helpful in your family discernment with your future spouse? Make that prayer your own.

Lord, help me abide with you in this season of engagement. In the hectic rush of wedding planning, help me to rest close to your heart and hear your voice. Strengthen me to entrust my maternity and future family to your will.

HOW MARY CAN
HELP YOU

*"We shall not be asked to do more than the Mother of God.
We shall not be asked to become extraordinary or set apart
or to make a hard and fast rule of life or to compile a manual
of mortifications or heroic resolutions. We shall not be asked
to cultivate our souls like rare hothouse flowers. We shall
not, most of us, even be allowed to do that. What we shall
be asked is to give our flesh and blood, our daily life — our
thoughts, our service to one another, our affections and
loves, our words, our intellect, our waking, working, and
sleeping, our ordinary human joys and sorrows — to God."*

— Caryll Houselander

If there was ever a human being who had marriage and maternity figured out, it was the Blessed Virgin Mary. Conceived without sin, im-
maculate, gentle, and kind, she dedicated her entire being, even her
virginity, to God.

Then God turned her world upside down.

At the Annunciation, God invited Mary to say "yes" to maternity, to become the Mother of God. She answered with the famous declaration of ultimate sacrifice and love: "I am the handmaid of the Lord; let it be to me according to your word" (Lk 1:38).

Then, after her fiat, her maternity and marriage were perfect, right? Actually, quite the opposite.

Soon after she proclaimed her Magnificat, her betrothed decided to quietly divorce her, until the angel set him straight. Then, she joined Joseph on a grueling, ninety-mile journey to Bethlehem. When they arrived at their destination, there was no room in the inn, so Mary had to give birth in a stable. After Jesus was born, the only place to lay him was a manger — and not a romanticized, nativity scene manger, but an animal feeding trough made of clay and straw, held together with mud.

As if her son's entrance into the world wasn't difficult enough, over the next thirty-three years Mary watched her child grow up to be an amazing teacher and healer. But despite his goodness, he was slaughtered by the Roman Empire on the cruelest torture device of the day, a cross.

When Mary said "yes" to God's will, the result wasn't perfection. The result was actually messy.

When we give our lives over to God in total surrender, our marriage and our maternity aren't guaranteed to be picture-perfect. Things may fall into place during some seasons; and in others, it will seem as if it's all falling apart. Sometimes, God will turn our world upside down, and we'll find that only then are things right where they should be.

God never promises perfection when we give our lives to him. In fact, he warns us explicitly that our lives will more than likely become harder, not easier, when we give ourselves completely to him. He says we will be persecuted for the sake of righteousness.

But do we want picture-perfect? Do we want the pristine manger scene of marriage and maternity, complete with clean straw and soft swaddling clothes? Do we want to ignore the messy reality of life?

When you ask that God's will be done in your marriage and for your future family, it doesn't mean that everything will magically fix itself. Instead, God will give you opportunities to trust him.

Look at the story of Mary. She'd pledged her virginity to God, and her gift was transformed into something that humans deem impossible: a virgin birth. God honored Mary's gift to him; yet, his plan for her life was vastly different than she could have ever imagined. After all, it's not often that you pledge your virginity to God and the result is a baby boy, the Son of God.

How often do we give God a gift of ourselves with a secret plan in the back of our minds about how he should use that gift?

God yearns for our trust more than anything. He desires to take the pen from our hand and write the most amazing, beautifully messy story with our lives — more beautiful than we could have ever written ourselves. He doesn't promise perfection. Yet he tells us that he will be right beside us — yes, even until the end of the world.

It won't be perfect. But it will be holy.

Lord, inspire me to turn to you and your mother in the future, when marriage or motherhood is messier than I expected. In those times when things are less than perfect, remind me that you are a good Father. Turn my expectations upside down and help me embrace the beautiful mess that ensues.

LITTLE MISSION FIELDS

*"Miss no single opportunity of making some small sacrifice,
here by a smiling look, there by a kindly word; always
doing the smallest right and doing it all for love."*

— Saint Thérèse of Lisieux

In the months leading up to my wedding, Saint Thérèse of Lisieux
kept following me. Friends mentioned that they were interceding to
her for Joseph's and my upcoming wedding and marriage. Prayer cards
with her image kept popping up in the adoration chapel and at the back
of church.

But even though everyone loved Saint Thérèse, I struggled to connect with her. Maybe it was her neatness. Her gentle smile that seemed
to find me in every chapel that I went to, a stray holy card there, a statue
here, this constant presence of roses. She was the epitome of humility,
and lived most of her life in a Carmelite convent. Thérèse was tidy and
calm, and I was internally wrestling and externally the definition of chaos. Meanwhile, on my way to the altar, I was struggling with my biggest
vice: pride.

But gradually, as more and more of my friends sang the praises of

Christ working through Thérèse in their lives, I realized that I needed to give her another chance — or rather, stop shutting off my heart to what Christ was trying to tell me through her.

Then I realized why I didn't get along so well with Saint Thérèse. She challenged me too much. There I was, looking at these lofty goals, these high aspirations for my marriage, my future family, my path.

All the while, Saint Thérèse smiled at me, inviting me to take a closer look at the little things. The little moments of wedding preparations that I wanted to blow through in my rush to get to the end of the countdown.

Saint Thérèse of Lisieux invites us to reexamine our mission.

Too often, I looked at my life through a wide lens. But Thérèse was sitting beside me, nudging my finger on the zoom button of that camera, constantly pulling my vision closer and closer to the individuals who were closest to me. My soon-to-be husband, my family, my dear friends. She kept saying that they were my mission — right in my backyard.

I didn't want to have a thing to do with that. That was personal. Messy. Sticky. No glory there, I thought. She kept proving me wrong — if only by her patronage. Thérèse, the Little Flower, who went into a cloistered convent, is the patron saint of missionaries.

Is this to say that God isn't asking big things of you, or that he doesn't have a big mission in mind for your future marriage and future family? No.

But your mission field, at least at the start, may look a lot like the dinner table at your house, or the desk at your office. It may look like a 2:00 a.m. conversation with a friend who needs to know that she's loved, or in honest and vulnerable conversations with your future spouse. Maybe it means taking a moment to pause, and see where the Lord is inviting you to dive deeper into spiritual maternity, or to prepare your heart for physical maternity.

"Our Lord does not look so much at the greatness of our actions, nor even at their difficulty, but at the love with which we do them," Saint Thérèse of Lisieux wrote. What small, daily mission is the Lord offering you in this season of engagement? Spend time reflecting on his mission for you.

Lord, open my eyes up to the mission that you're calling me to. Help me embrace your call to those little missions — the nitty-gritty daily life where I can serve others and in turn, serve you. Stop me in my busyness and inspire me to see you in even my daily tasks.

SACRIFICE OF
MATERNITY

"Maternity is a natural Eucharist."

— Archbishop Fulton J. Sheen

Parenting is an invitation to sacrificial love; but this is especially true
for women.

"Although both of them together are parents of their child, the woman's motherhood constitutes a special 'part' in this shared parenthood, and the most demanding part," Pope Saint John Paul II wrote in *Mulieris Dignitatem*. "Parenthood — even though it belongs to both — is realized much more fully in the woman, especially in the prenatal period. It is the woman who 'pays' directly for this shared generation, which literally absorbs the energies of her body and soul. It is therefore necessary that the man be fully aware that in their shared parenthood he owes a special debt to the woman."

As soon as you see those two little lines on a pregnancy test, you begin a season of sacrifice. As a mother, you'll literally give your very body to the baby growing inside of you. Morning sickness, stretch marks, and long nights all speak to the sacrifice of maternity. You'll give up comfort, sleep, and your favorite foods for this little person.

Even though maternity is beautiful, not every moment is elegant and glamorous. It's challenging. Littles bring messy rooms and dirty clothes, exhausted evenings and tighter budgets. Mothering is a constant invitation into sacrificial love.

Physical motherhood stretches us as women, too. Even if stretch marks don't spread across your belly, stretch marks can appear on your heart as you love those in your life. The greater our capacity for loving those around us, for being a place for them to unfold, the greater our capacity for suffering with them, and because of them. Love stretches our heart.

But we're not alone in this invitation to sacrificial love. At every Mass, Christ comes alongside us with the words, "This is my body, this is my blood." Christ offers his body and blood for us. As women we offer our own body, our own blood, for the growth of these little babies.

From the moment of that positive pregnancy test, motherhood is an invitation to totally give ourselves. As women, we can unite our maternity to the Lord — including his suffering, his death, his complete and total gift of self, and his Easter joy.

In these moments before you enter into your new vocation of marriage, spend time uniting yourself to Christ on the cross. Your marriage will be full of opportunities to sacrifice for the good of your spouse, and maternity (physical or spiritual!) will create this space, too. But Christ redeems our sacrifice, and comes beside us in our suffering.

Copy out and pray through the words of consecration from the Mass, and reflect on what they mean for you as a woman with a call to beautiful, authentic maternity.

Take this, all of you, and eat of it,
for this is my Body,
which will be given up for you.

Take this, all of you, and drink from it,
for this is the chalice of my Blood,
the Blood of the new and eternal covenant,
which will be poured out for you and for many
for the forgiveness of sins.
Do this in memory of me.

_____

_____

_____

_____

_____

_____

_____

_____

_____

_____

_____

_____

FRONT PORCHES AND DOMESTIC CHURCHES

"Marriage is an act of will that signifies and involves
a mutual gift, which unites the spouses and binds
them to their eventual souls, with whom they make
up a sole family — a domestic church."

— Pope Saint John Paul II

Perhaps it's because my love language is physical touch, but I love the tangibility of our Catholic faith. Some of my favorite Masses during the year are those celebrated with all of the smells and bells of Catholicism. I love watching the candles flicker during the Easter Vigil, smelling the incense, hearing the chanted hymns, reveling in the beauty of the Word made Flesh through the Eucharist.

Throughout the whole liturgical calendar, we're able to experience the embodied faith of Catholicism. The Rosary invites us to pray with our body and our soul. Sacraments themselves are outward signs of inward graces. And gloriously, the source and summit of our faith is the celebration of the Eucharist — a God who enters our earthly messiness and invites us to consume his body and blood, to interact with him in a real, raw, and tangible way.

Even the building of Catholic churches themselves speaks to this tangibility. Catholic churches aren't supposed to look like coffee shops or stadiums, because the Church calls us into something radically, earth-shatteringly beautiful — a relationship with God. That's why we build architecture that calls our hearts and souls upward and inspires awe at the ultimate beauty of God.

In our worship, the Catholic faith is made physically accessible, from the sacraments — like your upcoming wedding — to the soaring heights of cathedral ceilings. But that tangibility is not reserved just for Sunday, or for your wedding Mass. We should sense the same human reality of our faith when we enter the family home, the domestic church.

"Thus the little domestic Church, like the greater Church, needs to be constantly and intensely evangelized," Pope Saint John Paul II wrote in *Familiaris Consortio*. "Hence, its duty regarding permanent education in the faith. ... The family, like the Church, ought to be a place where the Gospel is transmitted and from which the Gospel radiates ... the future of evangelization depends in great part on the Church of the home."

You and your spouse are called to give your entire lives to Christ and his Church — not just on Sundays for an hour. You're called to eat, sleep, and breathe with Christ, even in those moments when you're folding the laundry, driving to work, helping a child into his or her pajamas, or chatting with your spouse at the end of the night.

Saint Teresa of Ávila once said that "God walks among the pots and pans." But I'm pretty sure that he strolls among all of the aspects of our daily lives, not just the kitchen tasks. We encounter God in our worship at Mass, but we also teach and learn his lessons of humility, love, and mercy within the four walls of our own homes.

When my husband and I were first married, we moved everything we owned into a one-bedroom apartment that we learned to call home. But before we moved in, we hunted for the right place to live. We looked at maps to find the best commute and sifted through floor plans. On a sticky note, we wrote down things that we were looking for in a home.

We looked for a kitchen that was open to the rest of the house, and a front porch where we could sit out on rocking chairs. We had our fingers crossed for a cozy fireplace that we could sit around with friends.

But when I took a closer look at our future home wish list, I realized that behind all of my wishes lay a desire to build a domestic church.

Why do I want an open floor plan that allows for conversation between the dining room and the kitchen? When we have friends and family over, I don't want them to feel shut off from the kitchen while we prepare dinner.

Why was a beautiful front porch area, with space for sitting in rocking chairs, on our list? I loved the idea of how front porches foster intentional community (especially with new neighbors).

Why did we want a homey front room with a welcoming fireplace? Joseph and I love spending time with each other playing board games, and inviting friends to join us on weekend evenings. During the winter, we lit the fireplace and spent quality time together in our cozy front room, having heart-to-heart conversations about our life.

As you prepare for this new season of life, you too may be moving to a new home. But a beautifully important part of this new home is the fact that you and your spouse are going to be building a domestic church, a family, together.

The Catholic Church calls us to a tangible faith life within our home. Our homes should be ablaze with love for God. It's within these homes that we encounter our brothers and sisters in Christ, and live out our vocation.

How can you make your new home a domestic church? What beauty and ritual can you bring into this new house, this new home, this new family? Spend time reflecting.

Lord, I want our home to be a place where people encounter you. Set my future marriage on fire with love of you and love of your Church. Equip our future home to be a place where you are honored, where others are seen

and loved, and where anyone who encounters our family is able to see your love reflected in our lives.

_____

_____

_____

_____

_____

_____

_____

_____

_____

_____

_____

_____

_____

YOUR MATERNITY
IS GOOD

"The 'revelation of the body' helps us in some way
discover the extraordinary nature of what is ordinary."

— Pope Saint John Paul II

Do you struggle to see your body, your maternity, and your fertility as beautiful and good? Sister, you are not alone.

Viewing our feminine bodies and fertility as good and holy is challenging enough in today's world. But the Catholic Church challenges us to view our bodies as not just good, but sacramental. A sacramental view means that we see our bodies as something created to express our love of God and his love for us. Our bodies are an icon of the Father, an icon of the beauty of heaven that is to come.

As a woman, your body makes visible what is invisible — receptivity, sensitivity, generosity, maternity. Even though some days it may not feel like it, your body is the perfect package for your unique personhood as a woman and as a daughter of God.

Pope Saint John Paul II devoted 129 Wednesday audiences to defin-

179

ing what he called the "Theology of the Body." In those lectures he said that "the body, and it alone, is capable of making visible what is invisible: the spiritual and the divine. It was created to transfer into the visible reality of the world the mystery hidden since time immemorial in God, and thus be a sign of it."

Do you struggle with healthy body image, or even the concept of seeing the body as sacramental?

"It's splendid because without our body, we couldn't communicate to those around us our joys and sorrows, thoughts and desires. We couldn't — with a glance, a touch, a word — make the beauty and complexity of our soul known," writes Emily Stimpson Chapman in her book *These Beautiful Bones: An Everyday Theology of the Body*.

"Without our body, we also couldn't love. We couldn't hug our children or kiss our aging parents. We couldn't touch the faces of the dying or gaze with sympathy at a woebegone co-worker. We couldn't bake birthday cakes for our best friends, paint shelters for the homeless, or knit scarves for our nieces and nephews," she continues.

Our bodies are good, holy, and sacramental — everything about our bodies teaches us something about who God is. This isn't something that's confined to an abstract conversation, though. "The theology of the body is a theology for the rooms where we make love," Emily continues. "But it's also a theology for the rooms where we work, where we eat, where we laugh, and where we pray." The sacramental worldview, understanding that our bodies point to the beauty of heaven to come, impacts every aspect of our lives.

Together with the body of your husband, when you make love as a married couple, you witness to the truth that God himself is a communion of persons. Because God gives himself to us in the Trinity in a total gift of self-love, our love must also be a total gift of ourselves. This is why the Church is against artificial contraception — it hinders our bodies from sacramentally expressing the beauty of a God who gives himself in total self-donation.

Does the idea of seeing your body as sacramental lead to more frustration than rejoicing or praising God for his creation? Does your fertility cause you more anxiety than peace, more hardship than joy?

It's true that you won't be able to do a complete lifestyle or body image change in a single day. Instead, today, commit to taking small daily steps to recognize the beauty of your womanhood and your maternity. Maybe that means getting rid of negative voices and inspiration that are clouding your social media feeds, or stopping yourself the next time you critique your body and complimenting yourself instead.

You're not alone in this battle, either. If you're struggling to see your body as good, surround yourself (in person and on social media) with women who are striving to see their bodies as good and holy. Write down some small steps that you can start incorporating into your day to help you recognize your body, especially your maternity, as good and sacramental.

Jesus, I'm surrounded by voices in this world that say that my fertility, my body, is a burden. I'm told that my fertility and maternity are problems to be fixed, not a beautiful gift to be cherished. Help me reject those voices and instead tune in to your voice, which sings that all of me is beautiful and good, especially the fact that you've created me as a woman. Inspire me to see myself the way you see me.

_____

_____

_____

_____

_____

_____

_____

_____

_____

_____

_____

_____

_____

_____

_____

_____

_____

_____

_____

_____

A GREAT CLOUD
OF WITNESSES

*"In this world two things are essential: life and friendship.
Both should be highly prized and we must not undervalue
them. Life and friendship are nature's gifts."*

— Saint Augustine

O n your journey to the altar and your ultimate journey to the Lord's
Sacred Heart, you're not alone. You're surrounded by friends and
family supporting you and your fiancé. This is so beautifully evident
at your wedding! But you're also being cheered on by a great cloud of
witnesses — the saints.

It's sometimes tempting to think of the saints as people who had it
all together. Maybe you've put the saints on pedestals, their shining ha-
los keeping them out of reach, friendship with them unthinkable.

But the saints aren't far out of reach, and not all of them are priests
and nuns who spent all their time praying. Sainthood isn't just for the
celibate!

"Every state of life leads to holiness, always! At home, on the street, at work, at church, in that moment and in your state of life, the path to sainthood has been opened," Pope Francis said. "Don't be discouraged to pursue this path. It is God alone who gives us the grace. The Lord asks only this: that we be in communion with Him and at the service of our brothers and sisters."

Many saints grew in holiness during the ordinary daily tasks of eating breakfast together, sweeping the floors, grocery shopping, loving their spouse, raising little ones, and ministering to others.

One of my favorite saints who was a wife and mom is Saint Zélie Martin. She was a loving wife and mom to nine children, one of whom grew up to be Saint Thérèse of Lisieux. She ran her own lace-making business with Louis, her husband. In a letter to him, she once wrote, "I am with you all day in spirit. ... I love you with all my heart, and I feel my affection doubled by being deprived of your company. I could not live apart from you."

Spend time in the upcoming days learning more about saints who were wives, saints who were mothers. Get to know Saint Monica, Servant of God Zita of Bourbon-Parma, Saint Gianna Beretta Molla, and Saint Elizabeth Ann Seton. Introduce yourself to Saint Anne, Saint Margaret of Scotland, and the Blessed Mother. Then ask these women to share in your stresses, joys, sorrows, and relaxation. Invite them to join you as you prepare for your wedding day.

These women have planned weddings, loved their spouses, raised little ones, and surrendered their entire lives to the Lord. Now they joyfully gaze upon the face of their eternal Lover, Jesus. That beautiful intimacy with the Lord is for you, too. Ask these women to help you in this season of engagement, in the upcoming season of marriage, and in a new season of maternity!

Lord, you've surrounded me with such a great cloud of witnesses to the beauty of Catholic marriage and of maternity. As I get closer to the wedding altar, I ask specifically for these women to join me in this journey. Let their example

of how they lived out the feminine genius in their ordinary, daily life inspire me not only in this season, but also in the marriage and maternity ahead of me. Remind me that I am never alone.

A MATERNAL EMBRACE

"The Church is a Mother because she is a Bride who is forever bringing forth children of light, pillars of holiness, sources of inspiration, challengers of truth, and defenders of the Faith."

— Mother Angelica

In the early days of the Church, Christians referred to the Church as a mother. Saint Faustus of Riez wrote, "We believe the Church as the mother of our new birth."

But what does it mean to say that the Church is a mother?

Mothers are nurturing, sacrificial, instructive, caring, supportive, wise, strong, and creative.

Just as mothers nurture new life, both within their bodies and for those with whom they interact, the Church nurtures. In the Church we're reborn through baptism and fed on the grace of the sacraments.

Mothers teach their children, and the Church also teaches and guides her children back to the arms of the Heavenly Father.

The Church is a mother — our mother. Even the architecture of church buildings calls our hearts and souls upward to this maternal reality. When Gian Lorenzo Bernini designed St. Peter's Basilica and the piazza that lies before it, he included columns that embrace visitors into the "maternal arms of Mother Church."

But the Church has no physical arms with which to scoop up her children, or feet to run to them when they cry out. She doesn't have physical ears to hear the voice of her children, or eyes to gaze on them lovingly.

Instead, it's through your maternal arms that the Church reaches out to embrace. Your feet can carry you as you journey alongside her children. Your ears can listen to the joy and sorrow of others, and your eyes can look on them with kindness.

This is the sanctifying maternity that Christ invites you into, sister. He invites you to throw your arms wide open, to hold nothing back, and to make a total and sincere gift of yourself. He beckons you into a transformative love that calls the Church's beloved children back to the heart of the Father.

It's what you were created for. You were created for love.

This reality isn't just an invitation for your wedding day, where you'll love your spouse, friends, and family through the beauty of your feminine genius. It's also an invitation to arms-wide-open loving in your marriage, the vocation you're about to enter into at the altar. There, you'll vow before God and those gathered to love each other in good times and bad, in health and in sickness, to love and honor each other all the days of your life. At the altar, you and your spouse will become a family.

Your marriage is a domestic church that should also have maternal arms that embrace those who interact with you. So throw open the doors of your home, your domestic church, and invite others into your family — but also, the greater family of the Church. There they can lay down their heavy burdens, and be embraced.

In your marriage, your receptivity, generosity, sensitivity, and maternity are offered as a complete gift of yourself. Your love can be a glimpse of the beauty of God, the Church, and of the universal call to sainthood.

How is God uniquely calling you to this arms-wide-open kind of loving?

Jesus, Lord, I'm drawing close to the day when I will stand at the altar with my future spouse, in front of you, present in the holy Eucharist. In your presence, I'll vow to give all of myself to my husband. Just as you gave your own body to your bride, the Church, help me to love my spouse entirely and sacrificially. Fill me with the grace I need for this vocation of marriage and help me reflect your divine life and love in the lives of all those I interact with. Let others see you and the beauty of Mother Church when they see our sacrament.

ABOUT THE AUTHOR

Chloe Langr is a freelance writer, blogger, and editor. She is passionate about the feminine genius and women's ministry, and is constantly inspired by Pope Saint John Paul II. The love of her life proposed to her on top of Emory Peak in Big Bend National Park in Texas, and they were married on January 21, 2017. When she isn't buried under a growing stack of books, you can find her climbing mountains, podcasting, and spending time with her husband, Joseph, and their daughter, Maeve. You can find more about Chloe on her blog, *Old Fashioned Girl*, and her podcast, *Letters to Women*.